TWAYNE'S WORLD AUTHORS SERIES
A Survey of the World's Literature

SPAIN

Gerald Wade

EDITOR

Pedro Antonio De Alarcón

TWAS 549

Pedro Antonio De Alarcón

PEDRO ANTONIO DE ALARCÓN

By CYRUS DeCOSTER

Northwestern University

TWAYNE PUBLISHERS

A DIVISION OF G. K. HALL & CO., BOSTON

First Printing

863
A 32 xd

Library of Congress Cataloging in Publication Data

DeCoster, Cyrus Cole, 1914–
Pedro Antonio de Alarcón.

(Twayne's world authors series : TWAS 549 : Spain)
Bibliography: p. 143–47
Includes index.
1. Alarcón, Pedro Antonio de, 1833–1891—
Criticism and interpretation.
PQ6502.Z5D4   868'.5'09   79-120
ISBN 0-8057-6391-0

81-3804

To David, Ken, and Jim

Contents

About the Author

Cyrus DeCoster was born in 1914 and brought up in St. Paul, Minnesota. He received his A.B. from Harvard in 1937. After spending a year studying at the Sorbonne, he did graduate work at the University of Chicago, where he was awarded the M.A. in 1940 and the Ph.D. in 1951. He taught at Carleton College from 1946 to 1957, at the University of Kansas from 1957 to 1969, and since then he has been at Northwestern University.

His special field of interest is Spanish peninsular literature of the nineteenth and twentieth centuries. He has published three editions of Valera's unpublished and uncollected works: *Correspondencia de don Juan Valera* (1956), *Obras desconocidas de Juan Valera* (1965), and *Artículos de "El Contemporáneo"* (1966). The Consejo Superior de Investigaciones Científicas brought out his *Bibliografía crítica de Juan Valera* in 1970. He edited Valera's novel *Las ilusiones del doctor Faustino* for the "Clásicos Castalia" series in 1970 and *Genio y figura* for Editorial Cátedra in 1975. His Twayne volume on Valera came out in 1974. He is currently working on an edition of Alarcón's uncollected short pieces. In addition, he has published articles, mostly on Valera, Pardo Bazán, Alarcón, and the contemporary theater, in various American and European journals.

Preface

Alarcón was a prominent man of letters, one of the leading novelists of the Generation of 1868, who also played an active role in politics. Yet it is not easy to draw a fully fleshed-out portrait of him. He remains an elusive figure, guarded in what he had to say about himself. Only a few of his letters have been published, and, for the most part, they are not very revealing. His prefaces and his *Historia de mis libros* (The Story of My Books) contain interesting, although occasionally contradictory, material about the genesis of his works, but they are not very informative about Alarcón the man. Nor are Alarcón's friends more helpful. Valera and Alarcón were, for example, on intimate terms for over three decades; yet Valera had rather little to say about his fellow Andalusian either in his letters or his critical writings. The editor Mariano Catalina, one of Alarcón's literary executors, wrote a biographical sketch which was first published in 1881 as a preface to the first volume *(Cuentos amatorios)* of his *Complete Works* in the "Biblioteca de Autores Castellanos" series. Later (in 1905) Catalina continued his study on up to Alarcón's death. Since they were close friends and Catalina certainly consulted Alarcón extensively, this has been considered the official biography, and subsequent critics have leaned heavily on it. It contains much information about Alarcón's life, but it is short on interpretation. Pardo Bazán, in her long necrological article originally published in the *Nuevo Teatro Crítico* in 1891, was the first to analyze Alarcón's works in some depth. Julio Romano's biography, *Pedro Antonio de Alarcón: el novelista romántico* (1933), is impossibly adulatory, as is Luis Martínez Kleiser's *D. Pedro Antonio de Alarcón: un viaje por el interior de su alma y a lo largo de su vida* (1943). Martínez Kleiser had access to the Alarcón family archives, and he quotes material which was not previously available. In his perceptive *Pedro Antonio de Alarcón* (1955) Montesinos concentrates on Alarcón's short fiction, and in the process presents an unenthusiastic, perhaps slightly biased, portrayal of Alarcón, the delayed Romantic. Armando Ocano's recent *Alarcón* (1970) is the best-rounded biographical study to date. But, all in all, we probably know less about him than about most of his contemporaries of comparable stature.

For the reader who knows little Spanish, I have translated the titles of Alarcón's works, usually where they first appear, unless they have easily recognizable cognates. The translations of the passages from Alarcón's works are mostly mine, although I have consulted and made use of Harriet de Onís's version of *El sombrero de tres picos*, Philip H. Riley and Hubert James Tunney's of *El escándalo*, and Robert Graves's of *El Niño de la Bola*. The page numbers in parentheses in the text refer to Alarcón's *Obras completas*, 3rd ed. (Madrid: Fax, 1968). Luis Martínez Kleiser's biography was reprinted as an introduction in that edition of the *Obras completas*, and the page numbers of references to this study are also given in parentheses in the text. Elsewhere in the Notes, *Obras completas* is abbreviated *O.C.*

I want to express my warm appreciation to my wife, Barbara, and to my daughter, Janine, both of whom spent many hours painstakingly going over the entire manuscript.

Chronology

1833 March 10: born in Guadix, province of Granada.

1847 Enrolls in the Law School of the University of Granada.

1848 Abandons the study of law for financial reasons; begins to study theology at the seminary in Guadix.

1852– Publishes *El Eco de Occidente* in Cádiz in collaboration with
1853 Torcuato Tárrago. Travels to Cádiz and from there to Madrid.

1854 Moves to Granada taking *El Eco de Occidente* with him. Member of the *Cuerda granadina*. Leads the rebellion against Sartorius in Granada and founds the anticlerical paper *La Redención*. Moves to Madrid in November.

1855 Takes over the editorship of the liberal daily *El Látigo*. February 12: duel with Heriberto García de Quevedo. First visit to Paris in May. Reworks and publishes *El final de Norma*.

1855– Writes extensively, publishing stories, sketches, and articles
1859 in various periodicals.

1857 His play *El hijo pródigo* gives rise to a polemic.

1859– Four months as war correspondent in Africa. *Diario de un*
1860 *testigo de la Guerra de Africa*.

1860– Six months traveling in France and Italy. *De Madrid a*
1861 *Nápoles*.

1861– Years devoted largely to politics.
1874

1865 Marriage to Paulina Contreras Reyes.

1866– In exile in Paris and Granada.
1868

1870 *Poesías serias y humorísticas*.

1871 *Cosas que fueron* (sketches).

1874 *La Alpujarra* and *El sombrero de tres picos*.

1875 *El escándalo*.

1877 Delivers his academy discourse "La moral en el arte."

1880 *El Niño de la Bola*.

1881 *El Capitán Veneno*. Begins to publish his works in the "Colección de Escritores Castellanos."

1882   *La Pródiga.*
1884   *Historia de mis libros.*
1888   November 30: suffers first stroke.
1891   July 19: dies in Madrid.

CHAPTER 1

Life

I *The Youthful Years*

GUADIX, Alarcón's birthplace, is located some thirty-five miles east of Granada in the foothills of the Sierra Nevada overlooking a fertile plain. It has a venerable past. The ancient Acci of the Romans, it was an important city during the Moorish occupation and was finally reconquered by Ferdinand and Isabel in 1489. Alarcón came from a distinguished family. One ancestor had taken part in the conquest of Granada; another had been charged with guarding Francis I after the French king was taken prisoner at the battle of Pavía in 1525. More recently, his paternal grandfather had been imprisoned for opposing the entry of the Napoleonic forces into the city.

But Guadix, like Alarcón's own family, had fallen upon trying times. Madoz in his *Diccionario geográfico de España* describes it as it was in Alarcón's youth (1847).[1] Of its 10,000 inhabitants, a third lived in caves. The streets were badly paved; the Alcazaba was in ruins; the town's four elementary schools were in ill repair. In Alarcón's *De Madrid a Nápoles* there is a similar evocation of Guadix as an impoverished agricultural city whence the well-to-do had fled to Granada or Madrid. Of Guadix's past grandeur there remained only the cathedral, an imposing transitional structure with Baroque details plastered on the original Gothic plan.

In this city Alarcón was born on March 10, 1833, the fourth of ten children. Martínez Kleiser quotes from a notebook in which Alarcón at some undetermined later date jotted down biographical details.[2] He precociously started school at three and a half. He began the study of Latin at nine, that of philosophy two years later, and at fourteen, after passing the examinations in Granada, he received the title of *bachiller* (bachelor).

Three of his *costumbrista* (regionalistic) sketches contain reminiscences of his youth in Guadix. In "La nochebuena del poeta" (1855) he nostalgically evokes the first Christmas Eve he was allowed to stay up, at the age of seven, and how superior he felt to his younger siblings when they were sent off to bed. The whole family gathered around the fire, the two grandmothers, the parents, the older children, and the domestic help with the men standing and the women kneeling or squatting. They sang Christmas carols, and Alarcón recalls one in particular sung by his paternal grandmother which impressed him with the inexorable passing of time and the inevitability of death: In spite of his youth, his heart froze.

La Nochebuena se viene,	Christmas Eve comes;
la Nochebuena se va,	Christmas Eve goes;
y nosotros nos iremos	And we will go off,
y no volveremos más.	And never return. (p. 1673)

In "Mis recuerdos de agricultor" (My Remembrances as a Gardener, 1880) Alarcón describes the garden which he and his nine brothers and sisters cultivated as children, each with his own small plot of land. Again the sketch ends on a sentimental note. One brother died. The others, one by one, moved away until only the parents were left to care for the garden, and then they, too, passed on. He himself has become a grown man with children of his own.

"Un maestro de antaño" (A School Master of Long Ago), one of Alarcón's most delightful pieces, was no doubt based on an actual person. The master, Sergeant Clavijo, a retired cavalryman, although eccentric and not well educated, was basically a very compassionate person whom he remembers with affection. Alarcón details the punishments he handed out, the faulty geography he taught, concluding with the hilarious horseback riding lessons. At a command of the sergeant the boys would jump up and straddle the high and narrow desks and pretend they were charging, in the process sending the books and papers flying and staining their pants with ink.

In October 1847, Alarcón began to study law at the University of Granada, but his family, with ten children to educate, could ill afford the cost. The priesthood seemed like a promising career for an intelligent youth, and the following January he enrolled in the seminary in Guadix. He had little calling for the clergy and eventually dropped out. During these years he read widely and indiscriminately, devouring everything he could lay his hands on, but his formal education was haphazard. Latin was the only foreign language he officially studied. He taught himself French and Italian without dictionaries or grammars, the former by comparing French and Spanish translations of Tasso's *Jerusalem Delivered*, the latter by comparing an Italian translation of the *Aeneid* with the original (p. 1900). This is hardly the easy way to learn a language! Judging from a sentence included in a letter to his brother Joaquín written while he was in exile in France in 1867, his knowledge of French, at any rate, was sketchier than he claimed: *A present je parle et je ecri le français comme si j'etais senateur de l'Empire* (p. xxi). It should read: *A présent je parle et j'écris le français comme si j'étais sénateur de l'Empire* (At present I speak and write French as though I were a senator of the Empire).

Alarcón felt more attracted to literature than to theology, and he was constantly writing. In 1848–49 he composed four plays in verse, including a historical drama, *La conquista de Guadix*. They were put on by amateur groups in Guadix but have not been preserved. From that same year dates his first work in prose, "Descubrimiento y paso del Cabo de Buena Esperanza" (Discovery and Passage of the Cape of Good Hope), a chronicle of the voyages of discovery in Africa ending with Vasco da Gama, which has come down to us.[3] The novel *El final de Norma* was also written at about this time. These youthful works indicate where Alarcón's true interests lay. Literature was to be his calling.

II *Expanding Horizons*

Opportunities in Guadix were limited; Alarcón was aware that he would have to go farther afield. He joined forces with Torcuato Tárrago, who was later to write countless mediocre historical novels and who was then living in Guadix. They found a wealthy sponsor in Cádiz to subsidize a literary journal. Thus, *El Eco de Occidente*, a weekly published in Cádiz and edited by Tárrago and Alarcón in Guadix, came into being in 1852. Here Alarcón published, in addition to poems and sketches, some of his first stories, including "El amigo de la muerte," "La buenaventura," and "El clavo." The journal, surprisingly enough, was a success, and Alarcón was encouraged. In January 1853, much against his parents' wishes, he left home, proceeding first to Cádiz and then to Madrid. He tried to find a publisher for his 2,000-verse continuation of Espronceda's unfinished philosophical poem *El diablo mundo*, but when he discovered that Espronceda's friend Miguel de los Santos Alvarez had just published his version, Alarcón philosophically burned up his own. Only nineteen and without connections, Alarcón found that opportunities were not opening up for him in the capital and that his money was running out. When his draft number came up, the prodigal son hurried home, and his family bought a replacement for him.

Later that year Alarcón went to Granada, and, beginning in January 1854, *El Eco de Occidente* was published there. He later reworked some of the pieces he wrote in Cádiz.and Granada and reprinted them in various Madrid periodicals. The intellectual climate in Granada Alarcón found congenial. He associated with a group of young writers and artists, who came to be known as the *Cuerda granadina*. They were so christened one evening when a group of them entered the theater holding on to each other to keep their balance as the space between the rows of seats was so narrow and someone cried out: ¡*Ahí va la cuerda*! (There goes the chain [of galley slaves]!). The individual members were called *nudos* (knots). They were young, high-spirited, bohemian, typical of the post-Romantic era in the lighthearted attitude they adopted toward life, art, and literature. They were full of high jinks. One evening they went about town serenading their *novias* (sweethearts) accompanied by four pianos which they carried along with them. In retrospect they are more picturesque than significant as a group. Alarcón was the only one to achieve a position of true stature. A few others—the orator José Moreno Nieto, the novelist Manuel Fernández y González, the poet Manuel del Palacio, the musician Mariano Vázquez, the Italian baritone Jorge Ronconi—came to occupy secondary positions; most of the rest have been forgotten.[4]

Alarcón, however, did take his politics seriously, and he became increasingly involved in the political struggles of the time. In June 1854, General O'Donnell rose up against the autocratic government. of Sartorius. After the indecisive battle of Vicalvaro in the outskirts of Madrid, a new government was set up under Espartero and with O'Donnell as Minister of War. When the news reached Granada, Alarcón became the leader of the uprising there. The rebels seized a supply of arms in the Alhambra, distributed them to the populace, and occupied the town hall and the headquarters of the militia. Alarcón founded a newspaper, *La Redención*, in which he published anticlerical diatribes.[5]

In the fall, after the rebellion quieted down, Alarcón moved to Madrid, giving up the editorship of *El Eco de Occidente*. Several of his Granada friends joined him there, and the *Cuerda granadina* became the *Colonia granadina*. They were joined by new recruits, including Antonio de Trueba, Agustín Bonnat, Núñez de Arce, and Mariano de Larra, the son of the essayist. The same carefree, bohemian attitude continued to prevail. Alarcón later evoked this period of his life in the introduction to two stories, "¿Por qué era rubia?" (1859) and "Sin un cuarto" (1874), and in the necrological article he published in 1884 about his old friend Gregorio Cruzado Villaamil. "¿Por qué era rubia?" (Why was she blond?) describes a sort of literary contest among six friends. They each are given half an hour to write a story with that title. Alarcón summarizes the other stories and then reprints his own. In the Introduction to "Sin un cuarto" (Without a Penny) some young men are confronted with the problem that they have only six *cuartos* between them. One wants the money to have his shoes shined so he can impress a politician; another, who has an appointment with a banker, for a shave; a third, for a stamp so he can write his *novia* in Granada. After a protracted discussion they decide that the third request is the most urgent.

But it was politics rather than literature that absorbed Alarcón during these months of his life. On November 1, 1854, the democratic newspaper *El Látigo* (The Whip) began publication in Madrid.[6] Each issue was called a *latigazo*, a lashing. Alarcón began contributing to the paper on December 9, first using the pseudonym *El Zagal* (The Postillion), and then later *El Hijo Pródigo* (The Prodigal Son). Early in January he took over the editorship, and his friend Manuel del Palacio joined him as chief collaborator. Alarcón attacked the standard villains of the liberals, Narváez and María Cristina, the Queen Mother, and he protested vehemently against taxes, conscription, graft, and capital punishment. His tone is irreverent, almost sacrilegious, as when he paraphrases the Beatitudes, the Creed, and even the Lord's Prayer to dramatize abuses in the government. His pungently bitter satire reminds one of Larra. This Alarcón has nothing in common with the apologist who twenty years later wrote *El escándalo*. In early February *El Látigo* was denounced to the censor and Alarcón was indicted. He

then became embroiled in a polemic with the Venezuelan Heriberto
García de Quevedo, who was writing for the conservative paper *El
León Español*. After being absolved of the indictment, Alarcón
wrote a particularly virulent article on February 10 attacking his
opponent. He began by addressing him *Al Valeroso Hidalgo Ul-
tramarino D. Quijote Segundo* (To the Valiant Knight from Over-
seas, Don Quixote the Second) and concluded by asking: "Why
don't you challenge us?" After this outburst a duel was inevitable.
They met on the twelfth of the month. Alarcón, a novice with
firearms, fired first and missed, García de Quevedo, an experienced
duelist, magnanimously fired into the air. Alarcón was badly shaken
by the experience. He later querulously blamed his fellow editors
for leaving him in the lurch, but it is difficult to see what they could
have done to aid him. He had certainly brought his troubles on
himself. In any case, he resigned from *El Látigo*, and the paper
expired of apathy later that month. Resolving never again to take
part in politics, Alarcón went off to Segovia for a month to lick his
wounds.

Except for occasional brief trips, Alarcón spent the next four and a
half years, until he left for Africa in late 1859, in Madrid. He
perfunctorily lists these trips in his "Cuadro general de mis viajes
por España" (General Outline of My Travels through Spain) and
describes a few of them in greater detail in articles later collected in
Viajes por España. In May 1855 he went to Paris for the Exposition,
his first foray outside of Spain, and described the trip in a series of
rather pedestrian articles in *El Occidente*.

Alarcón was now at the hub of Spain's intellectual and artistic life.
His horizons had broadened. He had access to the best periodicals
including *El Occidente, La Discusión, La América, El Museo Universal, El Semanario Pintoresco, La Ilustración*, and *El Mundo
Pintoresco*. The reworked manuscript of his youthful novel *El final
de Norma* was published in the *feuilleton* of *El Occidente* in the fall
of 1855. *El final de Norma* is impossibly melodramatic by today's
tastes, but it was popular in its day. He continued to cultivate the
short story, and several of his best ones, later collected in *Historietas nacionales*, date from these years: "El afrancesado," "El
ángel de la Guardia," and "El carbonero alcalde." He began to write
literary criticism, although only a few of these articles have been
collected. His early opposition to Naturalism is seen in his caustic
article on Feydeau's *Fanny*. He was the first in Spain to write about

Poe. After serving as drama critic, he decided to try his hand at play writing. *El hijo pródigo* was presented in November 1857, but it was savagely attacked by the critics, and he renounced writing for the theater. He took advantage of the active social life he was leading to write a series of social notes for *La Epoca* in 1858 and 1859. He collected many of the stories of these years in the three volumes of *Cuentos, artículos y novelas* (1859). Some of the articles were salvaged and published in subsequent collections, but many lie buried and forgotten in the periodicals where they first appeared.

In 1860 Alarcón had his first big journalistic success. The Liberal Union with O'Donnell as Minister had returned to power and embarked on an aggressive foreign policy, thus drawing the people's attention away from the country's pressing internal problems, in particular the deteriorating economy. In August 1859 some Berber tribesmen attacked a Spanish guard post near Ceuta in Morocco and defiled the Spanish flag. When O'Donnell's demands for redress were not fully met by the Moroccan government, Spain declared war on October 22, 1859.

Alarcón decided to go to Morocco to report on the war for the Spanish press. Among his fellow correspondents was the dramatist Núñez de Arce. Alarcón enlisted in the battalion from Ciudad Rodrigo and served as orderly under his friend and fellow man of letters, General Ros de Olano. Later, when O'Donnell took over command of the army, Alarcón transferred to his staff. Alarcón's jingoistic reports were enthusiastically received by the Spanish public. After returning to Madrid late in March, he published them in the two-volume *Diario de un testigo de la Guerra de Africa.*

Alarcón had acquired a measure of fame, and, more tangibly, the former student, who had been unable to finish his law studies because of lack of funds, was now financially well off. He resolved to make, at the age of twenty-seven, his grand tour. He left Madrid on August 29, 1860, and was gone just under six months. After spending a few weeks in Paris, he proceeded via Geneva to Italy, where he took in most of the country as far south as Naples. *De Madrid a Nápoles* (1861) is a detailed account of his trip.

III *Political Hiatus*

Alarcón later said in his *Historia de mis libros* that the first period of his literary life ended with *De Madrid a Nápoles* (p. 16). During the next nine years he published only one book, *Novelas*, a collection of short stories, which came out in 1866. He even contributed little to journals—a few poems and a dozen pieces in prose. This decade was primarily devoted to political activity.

When his friend and commanding officer in Africa, O'Donnell, still the leader of the Liberal Union, was forced to resign in 1863, Alarcón embarked on a campaign against his successor, Miraflores, in the pages of *La Epoca*. With Navarro Rodrigo and Núñez de Arce, he founded the Unionist paper *La Política*. He was elected deputy from Guadix and was returned regularly to the Cortes until finally defeated in 1872. In 1866 he signed the protest of the Unionist deputies, which resulted in his being exiled to Paris for a year. From there he proceeded to Granada, where, away from the maelstrom of politics, he did spend some time writing. The fine story "La Comendadora" belongs to this period. The Liceo of Granada awarded him a gold medal for his long poem "El suspiro del moro," and he began his novel *El escándalo*, although it was not finished until eight years later. After the Revolution broke out in 1868, Alarcón was present as an observer at the battle of Alcolea on September 18, in which the queen's supporter Novaliches was defeated by the insurgent forces under the command of Serrano. Alarcón returned to Madrid and was offered the position of minister to Sweden and Norway, which he turned down, preferring to keep his elective office of deputy and to remain at the center of action.

In June 1869 Prim became Minister, and a search was undertaken to find a successor to Isabel II. Alarcón first supported the candidacy of the Duke of Montpensier, the brother-in-law of the queen, in the Cortes and in *La Política* but without success. He wrote a pamphlet which was published anonymously, *El Prusiano no es España*, opposing the candidacy of Leopold de Hohenzollern-Sigmaringen. Leopold was offered the throne; he accepted but later withdrew his candidacy. Finally, in November 1870, Amadeo of Savoy was named king. Alarcón, opposed to any foreigner as monarch, published an article in *La Política* in 1871, "La Unión Liberal debe ser alfonsina" (The Liberal Union Should Support Alfonso [Isabel's son]). He was among the first of the Unionists to favor such a conservative step. After Amadeo abdicated in February 1873, a republic was established, which lasted less than two years, after which Alfonso was proclaimed king on December 29, 1874. The following month Alarcón was appointed Counselor of State in the Department of Public Works, the highest political office he was to hold. He was subsequently elected senator twice, but he never again took an active part in politics. As a politician Alarcón played a minor role. The youthful radical of *La Redención* and *El Látigo* became a political moderate in the 1860s. His later novels, *El escándalo* in particular, show him in an even more conservative light.

It was during this period of his life that Alarcón was married. Little is known about his amorous life prior to his marriage. Since he moved in the elite social circles and was a rising literary figure, we can imagine that there were women in his life, but he was reticent about them, quite the opposite of Valera, who wrote openly about his numerous affairs in his correspondence. Alarcón met his future wife, Paulina Contreras of Granada, in the summer of 1864 when he was thirty-one. He followed her to Almuñécar on the coast, where her family was vacationing, and they became engaged in September. They were married on Christmas Eve, 1865. It was to be a happy union, and Alarcón always spoke in very warm terms of his wife. Eight children were born of the marriage, three of whom died in infancy. His wife, who outlived him by thirty years, died in 1921.

IV *Later Writings*

In the next decade Alarcón began to devote more time to literary pursuits. He brought out several collections of short pieces which had previously appeared in periodicals. *Poesías serias y humorísticas* came out in 1870 with a prologue by Valera. *Cosas que fueron* (1871) is a collection of sixteen *costumbrista* sketches and "Revistas de Madrid." *Amores y amoríos. Historietas en prosa y verso* (1875), as the title suggests, contained both short stories and poems. In 1881–82 he published in the "Colección de Escritores Castellanos" what he considered the definitive edition of his short stories in three volumes, *Cuentos amatorios*, *Historietas nacionales*, and *Narraciones inverosímiles*. He gathered his most important articles of literary criticism in *Juicios literarios* and most of his short travel sketches in *Viajes por España* (both in 1883). *Ultimos escritos*, which came out posthumously in 1891, is a miscellaneous collection of critical articles, sketches, and poems mostly written during the last decade of his life. Clarín criticized Alarcón and/or his family for having allowed such inconsequential trifles to be published, and he quoted one particularly unfortunate poem.[7] Alarcón, had he still been alive, would have been incensed.

Alarcón reached the age of forty before he set out to make a name for himself as a novelist. (*El final de Norma* would certainly be forgotten today if he were not the author.) His contemporaries, too, were also slow in trying their hand at the major genre of the nineteenth century. Valera was fifty when he wrote *Pepita Jiménez* (1874) and Pereda forty-three when *El buey suelto* appeared in 1877. This delay is understandable, for the renascence of the novel was in part a product of the greater stability brought about by the Restoration. Alarcón's *El sombrero de tres picos* (1874) was an immediate success. He then set out to write a more ambitious work, an ideological novel exemplifying his conservative Catholic ideals, but the publication of *El escándalo* in 1875 created an uproar in the press. Irritated by this adverse criticism, for five years he wrote no more novels and, in fact, very little else. That same year he was elected to the Royal Academy, an honor which gratified him and helped assuage the bitterness he felt at the hostile reception of *El escándalo*. He did not read his academy discourse, "La moral en el arte," his most ambitious piece of literary criticism, until early in 1877, and it, too, provoked mixed reactions. In 1878 he bought a country home at Valdemoro in the outskirts of Madrid, and henceforth he divided his time between this estate and his apartment on Atocha Street in Madrid. In a letter to a friend he paints an idyllic picture of the bucolic life he led at Valdemoro and concludes: "In short, I am the true *tío* Lucas" (the protagonist of *El sombrero de tres picos*, p. xxix). Although his ultramontane views were less apparent in *El Niño de la Bola* (1880), it, too, was harshly reviewed. The next year *El Capitán Veneno*, a simple love story told in a humorous vein, was apparently well received by the public, although it was pretty much neglected by the critics. But when *La Pródiga* (1882), the story of an unconventional woman who comes to a tragic end, was also received largely in silence, Alarcón accused the critics of conspiring against him and renounced writing novels for good.

During the remaining nine years of his life Alarcón lived quietly, surrounded by his family. He traveled little and took almost no part in politics. He was seriously overweight and looked and acted older than his years. Pardo Bazán describes him when she met him for the first time in 1887. He breathed with difficulty; his eyes were listless; his face, expressionless; his complexion, pale and yellowish. Only when animated by the conversation, did he show what he had once been like.[8] His letters of these years show him as old, tired, and in ill-health, having lost his verve for living. In 1884 he said in a letter to a longtime friend: "How little fun is the autumn of life. We are all plagued by physical and mental illnesses. . . ." Three years later he wrote to one of his brothers: "You can't imagine how bad I feel, although I hide it from my family; these nervous disorders, to which we don't usually give any importance, are terrible when they are as bad as the ones I have been suffering for the past several months" (p. xxxi).

Actually, life had not treated Alarcón badly. He had achieved fame and popularity, and he had done well financially. But our thin-skinned Andalusian was sensitive to criticism and he was hurt by the adverse reaction to his three ideological novels. As he wrote in 1884 in *Historia de mis libros:* "An invincible sense of tedium as far as literary activitity is concerned took possession of me because of the meanness and discourtesy which are so prevalent" (p. 28). He abandoned fiction completely. The first part of his *Historia de mis libros* (1884) contains interesting comments about the genesis of his works; the last part degenerates into a never-ending series of querulous complaints. Otherwise, he wrote little during these years—a couple of prologues, a reply to Alejandro Pidal y Mon's academy discourse on Fray Luis de Granada, the sketch "Diciembre" for a luxuriously illustrated book, *Los Meses*. Alarcón was tired and had lost interest. His lethargy offers a marked contrast with Valera's activity during the last decade of his life when he was past seventy and blind. Alarcón no doubt sensed that he had not long to live. He suffered a series of four strokes, the first in November 1888, the last on July 15, 1891, and died four days later at the age of fifty-eight.

CHAPTER 2

The Critic

I Intellectual and Aesthetic Orientation

A LARCÓN was largely self-educated. The only advanced schooling he received was his theological training at the seminary in Guadix. Yet he managed to cover a good deal of literary ground. He had learned Latin as a boy and taught himself French and Italian. He was well-read in the classics; in his academy discourse, "Sobre la moral en el arte," he comments at some length on Greek and Latin literature. He also expresses his admiration for such universal giants as Dante, Shakespeare, and Goethe and shows familiarity with French literature of the seventeenth and eighteenth centuries. And, of course, he knew the Spanish classics of the Golden Age.

Alarcón belonged both chronologically and temperamentally to the post-Romantic era. He felt empathy for the writers of the previous generation: Rivas, Espronceda, and Zorrilla. While still in his teens he had written a continuation of Espronceda's unfinished *El diablo mundo*. He published a warm letter of welcome in *El Museo Universal* when Zorrilla returned to Spain from Mexico in 1866. But Alarcón was less interested in tragic love affairs laid in a medieval setting and did not cultivate the traditional Romantic novel or drama. Rather, he was attracted by those aspects associated with the second generation of Romantics—a predilection for the exotic, the macabre, the fantastic, and the facetiously humorous.

In his *Historia de mis libros* Alarcón mentions the writers whom he admired and who had influenced him, especially during the early years. The first stories, written in Guadix, were inspired by Scott, Dumas, Hugo, Balzac, and George Sand (p. 7). Then in the mid-1850s he came under the influence of the French humorist Alphonse Karr and his Spanish disciple, Alarcón's friend Agustín

Bonnat, one of the stalwarts of the *Colonia granadina*. Bonnat published humorous, fantastic stories in the journals of the time but is today virtually forgotten. It was his mannered, exaggerated style, in particular, that Alarcón imitated. He wrote a most laudatory article upon the occasion of Bonnat's premature death in 1858 (pp. 1785–88).

After outgrowing this youthful phase, Alarcón claims to have modeled his later stories on his current idols or "gods," Cervantes, Goethe, Manzoni, Quevedo, Goldsmith, Dickens, Shakespeare, and Byron. Scott and Balzac are repeated from the previous list. It is quite a mixed bag of names, and few examples of actual influence can be found in either his stories or novels. There are occasional passing references to Cervantes and Shakespeare in his work. *Tio* Lucas in *El sombrero de tres picos*, for example, is called an Othello from Murcia, but it is Byron who appears the most often. In an "Album de preguntas" (Album of Questions) of 1883 Alarcón lists him as the greatest poet (p. 1832), a rather surprising statement when one considers that Alarcón knew no English and had only read him translated into French prose. Fabián Conde in *El escándalo* is compared to a Byronic hero and La Pródiga also expresses admiration for him.[1] Scott had been extensively translated into Spanish and Alarcón was familiar with his novels, but since he never cultivated the historical novel, one can hardly speak of influence. He mentions Dickens only in passing, and actually he has little in common with the English novelist. Goldsmith is spelled both Goltmits and Golmichs. Unless these misspellings are errata, Alarcón was less familiar with him than he claimed to be.

Alarcón felt an affinity for French literature, especially during his early, francophile years. In 1855 he published a brief article describing a visit to the exiled Hugo's home in Paris.[2] He mentions Balzac as one of the strongest, early influences. In 1855 he made a pilgrimage to Balzac's tomb and later published an article, "La tumba de Balzac," in which he lavished praise on the French novelist and his *Comédie humaine*.[3] In 1858 Alarcón specifies that Balzac interests him "como anatómico, come fisiólogo, como psicólogo, como naturalista" (p. 1772). Alarcón had already tried his hand at writing *fisiologías*, as we shall later see. But rather than sensing the originality of Balzac as the first of the modern Realists, Alarcón prefers his early Romantic manner.[4] Somewhat surprisingly, nowhere does he name Gautier or Mérimée, with whom he had perhaps more in common than with Balzac. He had little sympathy for the French Realists and Naturalists, primarily on moral grounds, and Flaubert, Zola, and their followers are scarcely mentioned in his writings.

Alarcón was equally reticent about his contemporaries in Spain. Although he and Valera were friends of long standing, they never commented publicly about each other's novels. Valera did write an uncritically eulogistic prologue for the *Poesías serias y humorísticas* (1870). Alarcón dedicated the *Historietas nacionales* to his friend, and the latter, in turn, repaid the compliment in his *Apuntes sobre el nuevo arte de escribir novelas*. Valera's choice of the *Apuntes*, a sharp attack on Pardo Bazán's defense of Naturalism in *La cuestión palpitante*, was appropriate, as they shared a marked antipathy for the movement. Otherwise, they had rather little in common. Alarcón had almost nothing to say about Fernán Caballero, Pereda, and Galdós. By the time the second generation of novelists, Pardo Bazán, Palacio Valdés, and Clarín, came on the scene, he had virtually ceased writing.

II *Literary Criticism*

Alarcón wrote a good deal of literary criticism for periodicals during the late 1850s, a small part of which he later collected in *Juicios literarios y artísticos*. The papers carried only occasional articles about current books, but most of them had a regular drama critic. The theater was actually in a stronger position in Spain in the 1850s than the other genres. Alarcón reviewed plays at different times for *El Occcidente, La Discusión,* and *La Epoca*.[5] Many of these works were trivial potboilers which have long since been forgotten, but others were of greater stature. Alarcón tended to be a severe critic, and the fledgling dramatists were treated harshly. Even a major figure like Tamayo y Baus received his lumps. After speaking well of his *Hija y madre* and *Locura de amor*, Alarcón panned a production of *La bola de nieve*. The play lacked unity of tone: "It begins like a *sainete* [a one-act farce] . . . and ends in tears." The characters, he claimed, did not ring true, and the versification was faulty. He was equally hard on *Virginia*.[6] Other established dramatists usually fared better. In 1856 he praised La Avellaneda's *Alfonso Munio, Príncipe de Viana,* and *Saúl:* "One finds in these works the tranquil cadence, the grandeur, the majes-

tic sweep of true tragedy." Two years later he reviewed *Baltasar*
enthusiastically, going so far as to compare La Avellaneda to
Shakespeare, Calderón, and Hugo.[7] He also spoke favorably of
López de Ayala's *El tejado de vidrio*, in spite of the fact that it was a
zarzuela, a genre for which he felt antipathy.

Naturally enough, Alarcón often wrote about his friends. Special
mention should be made of the necrological articles on Agustín
Bonnat and his old Granada friend, José Jiménez Serrano, which
have a special poignancy, because both men died young with their
careers barely under way.[8] In 1856 he published a series of articles
about his companion from the *Cuerda* and *Colonia granadina*,
Manuel Fernández y González, discussing in considerable detail his
poetry and drama.[9] Alarcón devoted a long article to *De Villahermosa a la China*, the early psychological novel of his friend and
mentor Nicomedes Pastor Díaz. This is one of the few times he
wrote about a contemporary novel. In it he singles out the justifiedly
famous descriptions of nature which can be compared only to those
of Bernardin de Saint-Pierre and James Fenimore Cooper.[10] According to Montesinos, certain passages in *El escándalo* may well
have been inspired by *De Villahermosa a la China*.[11]

Two articles about foreign works are interesting because of what
they tell us about Alarcón's likes and dislikes. In 1858 he published a
scathing article on Ernest Feydeau's *Fanny*, which had had a *succès
de scandale* in Paris that year. The tightly written and hardly salacious confidences of a twenty-four-year-old man who is insanely
jealous of his thirty-five-year-old mistress's husband, *Fanny* is actually an original and perceptive work, which has been unjustly neglected by posterity. Flaubert and Sainte-Beuve appreciated the
novel's originality, although the more puritanical critics were
shocked by its adulterous theme. After conceding that the novel was
well constructed, Alarcón launched into a virulent attack on its
immorality. When he reprinted the article in *Juicios literarios y
artísticos*, he added a note saying that since he had written it
twenty-five years before, it proved his opposition to Naturalism was
of long standing. Alarcón is obviously using the term Naturalism in
an oversimplified sense, equating it with the sordid and ignoring
Zola's scientific and sociological theories. In the last piece he wrote,
the sketch "Diciembre" (1887), Alarcón claims that in France popular opinion is turning against "Zola, Goncourt, and the other corrup-

ters of good taste because the desired reaction against the vulgar, the indecent, the ugly, the pornographic, and the sordid has occurred" (p. 1890). One wonders how many of their novels he had read.

The second article on foreign literature concerned Edgar Allan Poe, who, understandably, struck a responsive chord in Alarcón. He had read Baudelaire's translation of Poe, *Histoires extraordinaires*, in 1858 and had published the first article about the American writer to appear in Spain. Alarcón borrowed from Baudelaire's introduction for his biographical sketch, likening him to Byron because of his brief and adventurous life. Alarcón was attracted by the fantastic elements in Poe's tales and praised him in particular for his "scientific, poetic spirit." In spite of this affinity, Alarcón was not directly influenced by Poe. "El año en Spitzberg," the most Poesque of his stories, was written in 1852, well before he became acquainted with him.[12]

Alarcón's most ambitious piece of literary criticism was his academy discourse, "Sobre la moral en el arte," which he delivered in February 1877. Written shortly after *El escándalo*, it expresses the same moralistic view of literature. Although we associate these conservative attitudes primarily with his three major novels, they formed part of his literary and philosophical credo almost from the beginning; witness his 1858 article on *Fanny*. His 1857 review of Manuel Ortiz de Pinedo's *Los pobres de Madrid*, an adaptation of a French play, expresses the same didactic view: "Dramatic works should be a lesson given by the author to the public so that it will learn to correct its vices, to curb its passions, to heal its soul, to console itself in times of grief, to hope and trust in the midst of the greatest injustices. . . . It is not enough to expose evil; a remedy must be offered" (p. 1781). This was precisely his goal two decades later in *El escándalo*.

In "Sobre la moral en el arte" he first expounds his theoretical position: just as he himself has always been guided by didactic goals, so should all creative artists, whether writers, painters, or sculptors. He goes on to state that the beauty of a work should enhance the goodness and truth of the ideas expressed. In equating the beautiful with the true and the good our post-Romantic is hearkening back to the neo-Classic aesthetic. We hear echoes of Boileau's *Rien n'est beau que le vrai* (Only the true is beautiful). Alarcón categorically rejects the theory of art for art's sake.

He then takes us on a rapid, chronological survey of art (mainly literature) from the Egyptians to modern times to illustrate his thesis. The major figures, Homer, the Greek dramatists, Pindar, Seneca, Vergil, Horace, Dante, Shakespeare, Cervantes, Goethe, and Byron, without exception receive praise. His puritanical bias causes him to condemn a few writers, Lucretius and above all Ovid among the Romans. Voltaire he criticizes for his "negative fanaticism," and he concludes by damning contemporary French literature, presumably the Naturalistic novels for their emphasis on the sordid, although he does not mention them specifically. After alluding to the Franco-Prussian War, he concludes on a self-righteous note: "Let us respect the grief of a humiliated nation and let us only ask that the harsh reparations which the Germans have imposed on them make them realize their past errors."

The liberal critics did not buy this conservative aesthetic. Revilla published a sharp rebuttal in the *Revista Contemporánea*, claiming it was "impossible to gather together in so little space so many errors." Among other things, he accused Alarcón of not understanding the meaning of the term art for art's sake and of not realizing that many forms of art—architecture, music, and usually painting and sculpture—can have no ethical concerns.[13] Clarín ridiculed Alarcón's discourse in two articles in the liberal paper *El Solfeo*.[14] He accused Alarcón of thinking that art for art's sake signified "the triumph of the International." He also made fun of Alarcón's summary survey of world literature, finding it hopelessly superficial. *El Solfeo* published another series of five equally adverse articles by Eladio Lezama and a caricature entitled "Los santos de ahora," in which Alarcón was represented in a cassock carrying a copy of *El escándalo* with the following caption: "An epidemic of bigots threatens the country; its leader, Alarcón."[15]

The small amount of other criticism Alarcón wrote during the last years of his life is of scant importance. His "Discurso sobre la oratoria sagrada" (1883), given in answer to Alejandro Pidal y Mon's entrance speech to the academy, is a conventional eulogy of the new member and Fray Luis de Granada. Prologues to a posthumous edition of the works of his friend José Selgas (1882) and to the poems of his former commandant in Africa, Ros de Olano (1886), are even more cursory.

Only for a few years in the later 1850s did Alarcón devote a significant proportion of his time to literary criticism. Although it was journalism, often hurriedly turned out to meet a deadline, he frequently comes off as a competent critic. Only when his moralistic prejudices intrude, as in the case of his article on *Fanny*, do his judgments seem biased; and in defense of Alarcón, it can be said that *Fanny* was pretty heady fare for that time. Except for the essay "Sobre la moral én el arte," in which he tried to expound his aesthetic credo in a logical fashion, his later pieces are of slight interest.

III   *Music and Art*

In addition to literature, Alarcón was genuinely interested in music, especially the opera, and in art. He made rather clever use of Bellini's opera in *El final de Norma* to develop the plot. The heroine is a singer and the protagonist a violinist and conductor. They fall in love while performing the opera, and the finale is sung several times at key points in the novel. In the late 1850s Alarcón frequently wrote in the papers about the current productions of operas by Rossini, Bellini, Meyerbeer, Donizetti, Verdi, and others. Similarly, when traveling through Italy, he regularly attended the opera (and the theater); his opinions of these productions appear in *De Madrid a Nápoles*. Rossini, whom, in the aforementioned "Album de preguntas," he called the greatest composer, comes off particularly well. When he was in Paris in 1860, his old friend from the *Cuerda granadina* Jorge Ronconi took him to a *soirée* at Rossini's home in nearby Passy, and Alarcón was delighted to meet the famous composer. On the other hand, he was surprisingly hard on Verdi in an 1858 review of *Macbeth*, ranking him far beneath Rossini, Bellini, and Donizetti. "Verdi is what costume jewelry is to gold and gems, what the French painters are to Titian, what parrots are to men. He is the Churriguera of music, the great corrupter, the counterfeiter of true feeling!"[16] The *zarzuela* he disliked, finding it vulgar and inane, and he deplored the fact that Spaniards neglected opera to devote their attention to that inferior genre.[17]

Alarcón reviewed the National Exposition of Fine Arts for different papers in 1856, in 1858, and again in 1868.[18] In these articles he comments briefly on the works exhibited, claiming to be only a layman in matters of art, more or less sensitive to beauty, but no expert. It was not an exciting period in Spanish painting, and the artists he discusses—Rosales, Madrazo, Haes, etc.—are pretty much ignored today. Of more interest are his travel pieces, "Dos días en Salamanca" and above all *De Madrid a Nápoles,* a great deal of which is devoted to describing the buildings and works of art he saw. He comes off as an informed amateur, which is what he considered himself to be. That Murillo was his favorite painter tells us something about his taste (p. 1832), but then that would have been a not uncommon view in nineteenth-century Spain. A good many of his contemporaries would also have preferred Murillo to Velázquez.

CHAPTER 3

Short Stories

BETWEEN 1852 and 1854 Alarcón wrote short pieces of all sorts for *El Eco de Occidente,* mostly stories, *costumbrista* sketches, and poems. I was unable to locate the issues of *El Eco de Occidente* published in Cádiz in 1852–53.[1] The first versions of the stories "El amigo de la muerte," "La buenaventura," "El clavo," and "La cruz de palo" appeared in it; what else, one cannot say. The issues published in Granada in 1854 were collected in a volume and are readily available.[2] Alarcón left Granada in July of that year, and after a month's hiatus, Salvador de Salvador took over the editorship of the journal, although Alarcón continued to send him material from Madrid. Alarcón salvaged six stories from the year's production, "El abrazo de Vergara," "El asistente," "¡Buena pesca!," "La corneta de llaves," "El extranjero," and "El rey se divierte," in addition to a few poems and republished them later. In 1924 Agustín Aguilar y Tejera collected the rest of Alarcón's production for that year, a miscellaneous grab bag of sketches, articles, poems, and one story which gave the title to the volume, *Dos ángeles caídos y otros escritos olvidados* (Two Fallen Angels and Other Forgotten Works).[3] Much of the material is hack work, hurriedly cranked out because copy was needed, and Aguilar did Alarcón's reputation little service by republishing it. The "lost" material of the Cádiz issues was, no doubt, equally trivial.

After establishing himself in Madrid, Alarcón reworked much of this material from *El Eco de Occidente,* particularly the stories, and published them during the late 1850s in various journals, principally *El Museo Universal,* the *Semanario Pintoresco Español,* and *La América.* At the same time he was also writing new material. In 1859 he collected ten stories, "El afrancesado," "El extranjero," "¡Viva el Papa!," "El ángel de la Guarda," "Dos retratos," "El asistente,"

"Los ojos negros," "El clavo," "Dos ángeles caídos," "Soy, tengo y quiero," and the sketch "Las ferias de Madrid" in three volumes of *Cuentos, artículos y novelas*.[4] In 1866 he republished some of these stories plus others in another collection, *Novelas*, which is today very rare.[5] The volume was, incidentally, well reviewed by Manuel del Palacio, who likened Alarcón to Balzac and Poe.[6] Five years later appeared *Cosas que fueron. Artículos de costumbres*. The subtitle is something of a misnomer because, in addition to *costumbrista* sketches, it includes travel articles and pieces of literary criticism, both new and old. Another volume, *Amores y amoríos, historietas en prosa y verso* (1875), contains mostly recent material which was being collected for the first time.[7]

In 1881 Alarcón began to publish his so-called *Obras completas* in the "Colección de Escritores Castellanos"; the last of the nineteen volumes finally came out in 1892. The short stories were collected in three volumes, *Cuentos amatorios* (1881), *Historietas nacionales* (1881), and *Narraciones inverosímiles* (1882). A revised edition of *Cosas que fueron* was brought out in 1883 with only *costumbrista* material. The travel articles plus the regionalistic sketch "La granadina" went into a new volume, *Viajes por España* (1883), while the articles of literary criticism were gathered in *Juicios literarios y artísticos* (also 1883).

We have seen that in his *Historia de mis libros* Alarcón divides his short stories chronologically into three groups. The first stories, written in Guadix and Granada, and including "El clavo," "El amigo de la muerte," "El extranjero," "El asistente," and "La buenaventura," supposedly show the influence of Scott, Dumas, Hugo, Balzac, and George Sand. The second group consists of the stories he wrote after coming to Madrid in 1854 when he had come under the influence of Alphonse Karr and Agustín Bonnat. In retrospect, he looks back on this fad of his as an aberration, and he characterizes such stories as "El abrazo de Vergara," "La belleza ideal," "Los seis velos," "¿Por qué era rubia?", and "Soy, tengo y quiero" as extravagant and buffoonish. In general, they are not among his strongest efforts. In the third group, which includes "La Comendadora," "La última calaverada," "Moros y cristianos," and "Tic . . . tac," he says he has renounced his "Bonnat" manner. These late stories, the work of the mature Alarcón, are consistently of superior quality.

The majority of Alarcón's stories were written in the 1850s, before he reached the age of twenty-seven. During the next decade he was primarily involved in politics and wrote rather little. "Novela natural" (1866) and "La Comendadora" (1868) were the only stories published during those years. When in 1873 he began to devote himself to literature again, he concentrated on the novel and wrote only a few stories: "La última calaverada" (1874), "Sin un cuarto" (1874), "Tic . . . tac" (1875), "El libro talonario" (1878), "Moros y cristianos" (1881), and "La mujer alta" (1882).

When bringing out new editions of his works, Alarcón almost invariably made revisions, often of a substantial sort. Montesinos has studied in detail the variants of many of the stories. In some cases there are as many as three different versions. For example, "El clavo" was first published in *El Eco de Occidente* in 1853; Alarcón revised it extensively when republishing it in the *Semanario Pintoresco Español* in 1856 and once again before collecting it in the *Obras completas*. Montesinos claims that although Alarcón often made minor stylistic improvements, the later versions are usually no better than the original ones: "The author is incapable of improving on his first draft. He can rewrite a work of his; what he cannot do is to redo it."[8] Montesinos, not a great admirer of Alarcón's, is somewhat hard on our novelist. Alarcón made no effort to alter the fundamental nature of his works when revising them, but at least the majority of his changes are for the better.

The division of the stories into the three volumes, *Historietas nacionales, Cuentos amatorios,* and *Narraciones inverosímiles,* is somewhat capricious. Some of the stories would seem to fit better in another of the collections, and several of the pieces are not even stories at all. But no grouping is altogether satisfactory, for there is just too much variety. So I shall follow Alarcón's divisions, which is what most critics, including Montesinos, have done. No other system seems preferable. I have, however, postponed discussion of those works which are really *costumbrista* sketches to the chapter where I take up this genre.

I   Historietas nacionales

Seven of the *Historietas nacionales* are war stories, mostly dealing with the War of Independence, hence the title of the volume. They are all early works, written prior to 1860. In three of the most popular of them, "El carbonero alcalde," "El ángel de la Guarda," and "El afrancesado," Alarcón glorifies the bravery of the Spaniards in their struggle against Napoleon. The chauvinistic tone, the improbably heroic exploits of the Spaniards, the barbarous deeds of the invaders, and the exaggeratedly rhetorical language are indicative of their Romantic affiliation. The protagonist of "El alcalde carbonero," the mayor of a village of charcoal makers near Guadix, leads the heroic if futile defense of the town by the vastly outnumbered peasants against a French army. At the end, surrounded and seriously wounded, he hurls himself to death on the rocks below to avoid being captured. "El ángel de la Guarda" is a true story according to Alarcón. The setting—Tarragona on an idyllic May day in 1814 after the departure of the French—offers an ironic contrast with the tragedy that occurred there during the invasion. Three years earlier a young couple with the woman's mother and baby brother, had taken refuge in a dry cistern. When the baby started to cry, the mother clutched him to her breast so the pursuing soldiers would not hear him. The three adults were saved, but the baby suffocated, and the mother subsequently lost her mind.

In "El afrancesado," García de Paredes, an apothecary and a descendant of the sixteenth-century hero of the same name, is accused of being an *afrancesado*, a French sympathizer, for consorting with the enemy. One evening, while he is hosting a banquet for twenty French officers, the townspeople break in, intent on killing him for his treachery. Instead, they find that he has poisoned the wine, and both he and the officers are about to expire. The final scene, with the townspeople supporting the hero surrounded by dead and dying Frenchmen, could scarcely be more romantic:

You would have then seen a tableau as sublime as it was frightful. Several women, seated on the floor, were holding the dying patriot in their laps and arms. Just as formerly they had been the first to demand his death, now they were the first to shower him with caresses and blessings. The men had taken all the lamps from the table and, kneeling, were lighting up that patriotic and charitable group. And at each death rattle which was heard, each time a Frenchman slipped down to the floor, a glorious smile lit up the face of García de Paredes. (pp. 115–16)

The townspeople react to García de Paredes's barbarous act of poisoning the enemy officers in cold blood with "a simultaneous cry of terror and admiration."

A. H. Krappe argues that the source of this story was an episode in the civil war between Caesar and Pompey as recounted by the Greek historian Appian.[9] The protagonist here was also an apothecary, and the number of officers poisoned was the same, which hardly seems coincidental. But one doubts that Alarcón had been that familiar with Appian. Fichter more plausibly suggests that many similar stories circulated in Spain during the years following the Napoleonic invasion and that Alarcón was simply retelling a traditional tale.[10]

"El extranjero" (The Foreigner) has quite a different slant. A Spanish soldier coldheartedly kills and robs a sick Polish prisoner named Iwa near Almería. Some years later he himself is taken prisoner and forced to join Napoleon's army invading Russia. He falls ill in Warsaw and is cared for by a Polish family. The mother recognizes a locket he is wearing as one that had belonged to her son, Iwa. She and her daughters gain revenge, brutally clawing him to death with their nails. The soldier thus pays retribution for his crime.[11] Alarcón here is critical of the inhuman treatment of helpless prisoners. The jingoistic tone of the other war stories is absent, and the villain is even a Spaniard. But the Romantic strain is still strong. It is a violent story, and the outcome depends heavily on coincidence; it is Iwa's family in Warsaw that happens to befriend the Spanish soldier. Alarcón uses two narrators in the story. The first episode is told the author by an old peasant, a miner, who had witnessed the murder of the Pole. Then a few days later the author overhears the second part being recounted by a retired army officer in the *casino* in Almería. This device, although not ineffective, is perhaps a little too neat.

"La corneta de llaves" (The Cornet) is the only one of the war stories with a humorous strain to it. An officer, captured by the Carlists, is about to be shot, but saves his life by volunteering for the band, claiming he can play the cornet. By practicing night and day for two weeks he manages to get by. However, once the war is over, he refuses to have anything to do with the instrument.

The rest of the stories are more heterogeneous. "La buenaventura" is, like most of the *Historietas nacionales*, supposedly historically true. It was first published in *El Eco de Occidente* in 1853 under the title "Parrón" (p. 10). A gypsy is captured by a band of thieves led by Parrón, the scourge of the district, who kills all his captives so no one can inform on him. The wily gypsy offers to tell Parrón's fortune, his *buenaventura*. His prediction is that the thief will be hanged the following month. Parrón says that he will keep the gypsy prisoner for a month and will then shoot him if the prophecy is false. The gypsy manages to escape and returns to Granada. There one day he recognizes Parrón as one of the local militia. So the thief is captured and hanged, just as the gypsy had foretold. Parrón acknowledges that he had been a fool to spare the gypsy's life and that he is getting what he deserves. The story has an authentically popular ring to it which explains why it has been frequently anthologized.

With its Andalusian setting and shrewd peasant characterizations, "El libro talonario" (The Stub Book, 1877) has something in common with "La buenaventura." The opening pages have a regionalistic note to them; Alarcón describes in some detail how the gardeners of Rota lavish care on their squash and tomatoes. *Tío* Buscabeatas (the name—Seeker of Bigots—is amusing but hardly appropriate in the story) finds one morning that his beautiful crop of squash has been stolen. He locates them in the market of nearby Cádiz. The device he uses to prove they are his is in the spirit of a *chascarrillo*, a humorous popular story. He had cut the stems off all the plants and is able to fit each into the irregular hole on the top of its respective squash, just as the tax collector tears receipts unevenly from his stub book so as to be able to ascertain later whether they are authentic. The thief is sent off to jail, and everyone compliments *tío* Buscabeatas on his ingenuity. Told in a simple and unpretentious manner, "El libro talonario" is one of Alarcón's most successful stories.

Other stories might as well have been included in one of the other two collections. In "Fin de una novela," which is dated Guadix, 1854, the narrator wanders into an abandoned and semiruined monastery in Guadix late one fall afternoon and comes upon a beautiful woman praying. When she sees him, she falls down unconscious. He flees and later discovers that she has died. No one knows anything about her past or why she was living there. As the title suggests, the author gives us the ending of the story but not the beginning. The setting, the time of day, the season, the mysterious situation, the fragmentary quality of the story—all contribute to creating a poetical mood.

"¡Buena pesca!", a violent and melodramatic tale of love, jealousy, and revenge, typifies another aspect of Romanticism. An elderly, unattractive fisherman is insanely jealous of his beautiful young wife. He is aware that she is interested in their neighbor, a hand-

some young noble, and he plans to do away with his rival. After
cutting partway through the log which serves as a bridge crossing
the stream to their cabin, he announces to his wife that he is
spending the night in town. Upon returning the next morning, he
finds the log broken through as he expected, but two bodies instead
of one are caught in the net he had strung downstream. By the time
the police arrive, he has gone crazy and is in the process of sawing
off his right hand. Alarcón makes little effort to analyze the
psychological motives of his characters. The story is even told with a
frivolous touch typical of his early Bonnat manner, which does not
jibe with the gruesome end. He contrasts the physical appearance of
the couple: "It is true that if the poor fisherman dressed shabbily, it
was because his wife did quite the opposite; it is true that if the
husband had worked less in order to care for his hands, she would
have had to work more, thus spoiling hers; it is very true that the
fish which smelled so bad paid for the soap which smelled so good"
(p. 144). The wife's incipient infidelity is treated banteringly, almost
as though he were writing a drawing-room comedy instead of a
grisly tale of passion and jealousy. Even the title of the story,
"¡Buena pesca!", the words the mad fisherman repeats as he saws off
his hand, have an ironic tone. His good catch is his dead wife!

II   Cuentos amatorios

Although there is variety in the collection *Cuentos amatorios*, the
stories all treat a common theme, love, in one or another of its
aspects. They range from the melodramatic "El clavo," to the Freudian "La Comendadora," to humorous tales such as "La última
calaverada," "Sin un cuarto," "La belleza ideal," and "Tic . . . tac."

"El clavo" (The Nail) is one of Alarcón's longer stories, over half
the length of *El Capitán Veneno*. In *Historia de mis libros* Alarcón
claims that "El clavo," which is subtitled "Causa célebre," a translation of the French *cause célèbre* (famous trial), was recounted to him
by a magistrate in Granada when he was a youth. It may well be
based on an actual event, but, as Alarcón tells it, it is a wildly
implausible tale. At first there appear to be five main characters, the
narrator, Zarco the protagonist, and three women, but then the
three telescope into one. The story opens with the narrator meeting
a beautiful and mysterious woman on a stagecoach, but they are
soon separated. A few days later, he goes to visit his friend Zarco,
the judge in a small Andalusian town. While walking by a cemetery,

they happen upon a recently disinterred skull with a nail driven through it. The victim turns out to be a prominent local citizen who had presumably died two years before of a stroke. The two friends realize that this man must have been murdered by his wife, Gabriela, who had been alone with him at the time. The judge vows to find the culprit.

Zarco describes to the narrator his complete disillusionment with women. He had fallen in love with a beautiful woman named Blanca while visiting Seville two years before. Although she had become pregnant by him, she refused to marry him then, but promised to meet him in Seville a month later. When he returned two weeks early, she was nowhere to be found. Disenchanted, he left and obtained a transfer to another town.

The narrator then goes to Seville, where he encounters his stagecoach friend at a ball. She claims to be a Spanish American named Mercedes, and again she vanishes. He returns to visit Zarco. Suddenly Blanca appears and explains that she had forgotten the name of the town where Zarco was stationed and had been unable to communicate with him until she met the narrator in Seville. Their illegitimate child had died at birth. Zarco is enraptured, for he has found the woman he loves. Then the police inform him that the murderess has been apprehended. In a dramatic confrontation they discover that Gabriela, Blanca, and Mercedes are one and the same person. When she left Seville the first time, she had returned home and murdered her husband, whom she loathed, in order to be free to marry Zarco. The incorruptible Zarco sentences her to death and leaves town. When three weeks later she is being led to the gallows, Zarco comes galloping up with her pardon, but at that very moment she dies, overcome by the strain.

One of Alarcón's most popular stories, "El clavo" has been reprinted and translated many times. It is understandable that mid-nineteenth-century readers would be carried away by the sensational plot. Alarcón manages to build up considerable suspense, but the story is full of improbabilities. Zarco happens to be assigned to the town where Blanca (Gabriela) had formerly lived. He chances upon the skull with the nail driven through it. It seems incredible that she had forgotten the name of the town where he lived so that she was not able to communicate with him or that he was able to obtain a pardon for her. On what grounds, one wonders. Numerous times in the story Alarcón invokes the hand of fate. He states that the upright judge was destined to discover the crime the woman he loved had committed, to sentence her to death, and then to arrive late with the unwarranted pardon. When, after finding the skull, the narrator asks Zarco whether Gabriela will be caught, he replies: "There is a certain dramatic fatality which never pardons. More explicitly: when bones come out of a tomb to testify, there remains little for the courts to do" (p. 67). The theme of passionate love, the series of fortuitous actions, and the role played by fate make "El clavo" one of Alarcón's most melodramatic stories.

"Novela natural" starts out as a Romantic tale and then ends on an ironic note. A girl finds a notebook in the Plazá Santa Ana in Madrid and, from the notes and comments in it, giving free rein to her imagination, she pieces together the troubled life of its owner, a young man beset by gambling debts and despairing of ever being loved. At that point her father comes in and tells her that the young man has just committed suicide in the Puerta del Sol. The "notebook" device is clever, but at the same time, artificial. At the end of the story the father tells the daughter to order the servants to put on dinner. Like the girl's father in Mesonero Romanos's sketch "El romanticismo y los románticos," who says: "And in the meanwhile the shirts don't get sewn and the house doesn't get swept, and all my money goes for books," he belongs to another generation and has little sympathy for the excesses of the young.

"La Comendadora," a work of the mature Alarcón, stands in a category apart among his stories, both in subject matter and technique. The setting is a palace in Granada in the eighteenth century. Three people are present. The grandmother, a proud and inflexible countess, had virtually forced her daughter, now an attractive woman of thirty, to enter a convent (belonging to the order of the Comendadoras of Santiago—hence the title) so that the family inheritance would go undivided to the older brother. The son had died, and the two women are caring for the grandson, a spoiled, high-strung, and neurotic child of six or seven. The boy announces that he has overheard a painter who is restoring art works in the palace say to a sculptor: "How beautiful the Comendadora must look naked! Like a Greek statue!" (pp. 34–35). The boy then insists on seeing his aunt naked. Throwing a tantrum and frothing at the mouth, he keeps shouting, "See her naked!" until the grandmother, fearing for his life, sends the servants from the room and tells her daughter, "It is God's will." That evening the Comendadora returns to her convent, never to leave again.

"La Comendadora" is psychologically the most interesting and original of Alarcón's stories. The domineering grandmother who had shipped her daughter off to a convent at age eight is manipulated by the unbalanced child. She hypocritically tries to pass the blame off on God and has the Inquisition take the unfortunate painter off to prison. In "La Comendadora" Alarcón has left behind his Romantic heritage. The story with its Freudian implications has a modern tone to it, and it is told with a sobriety and concision unusual in Alarcón. The brief yet evocative description of the luxurious palace on a sunny spring morning offers a contrast to the decadent, aristocratic family. The three figures are rapidly yet effectively characterized. The story builds up quickly to the climax—the succinct order the grandmother gives her daughter. What follows is left to the reader's imagination. Alarcón avoids all erotic titillation and soberly focuses on the psychological situation. There is no overkill, as in so many of his stories; he suggests more than he says.

The critics have been universal in their praise of "La Comendadora." Pardo Bazán, the first to write at some length about Alarcón's stories, appreciated its unique position: "It is impregnated with an inner melancholy, which takes hold of the soul. Here there is no *verdor gozo* [sexual stimulation], only black austerity."[12] The usually hostile Montesinos waxes enthusiastic and concedes that it is "one of Alarcón's rare unqualified successes."[13]

In several of the *Cuentos amatorios*, rather than exalting romantic love, Alarcón treats humorously the discomfiture of a suitor. These genuinely amusing stories lack the pretentiousness which mars much of his work. "La belleza ideal" and "El abrazo de Vergara" (The Embrace at Vergara), both early works (1854), are variations on the same situation. In the former, an ingenuous young man meets an attractive, somewhat older woman on a train. Discovering that he is a stranger to Madrid, she insists that he stay in her home. He is under the illusion that he is about to embark on an affair when he discovers that she and her husband run a pension and she was only after a boarder. In the second story, the narrator is seated next to a beautiful woman in a stagecoach. When he begins to court her and pay her extravagant compliments, she remains silent, leading him to think she is a foreigner and does not speak Spanish. He is finally about to embrace her when they pull into the Basque town of Vergara. She jumps out of the coach, greets her husband, and goes off saying good-bye to him in perfect Castilian.

Examples of his "Bonnat" manner remain in the later, definitive version of the story. The title itself is a pun, alluding as it does to the reconciliation between the liberals and the Carlists in Vergara in 1839. The relationship between the two episodes is, of course, ironical, for the protagonist in the story gets no embrace. The style is deliberately jerky, with a series of paragraphs each containing but one short sentence. Exaggerated metaphors call to mind Gómez de la Serna's *greguerías:* "The hand is the thermometer of love; the eyes are the barometer; and the heart the chronometer." "When four eyes of less than twenty-five say *tú* to each other, it is dangerous for them to keep looking at each other." Then Alarcón facetiously adds: "This axiom is composed of a phrase of mine, an allocution by Alphonse Karr, and a verse by Lord Byron" (p. 89).

A former rake tells the story of his reformation in "La Última calaverada" (The Last Escapade, 1874). One foggy night he left his home in the country on horseback to embark on an adulterous affair with a neighbor's wife. En route he fell off the horse, spent some time looking for his hat, and then proceeded on his way. Upon arriving at what he thought was his prospective mistress's villa, he found instead that he was back at his own house with his wife. After he had climbed back on his horse, the animal had headed for home without his realizing it. Taking this as a lesson, he renounced his philandering.

"Sin un cuarto," also of 1874, is the story of Rafael, a young, wealthy, and naive young man, who meets an attractive woman at a masquerade ball. She encourages the captivated but recalcitrant youth to accompany her home. He treats her like a lady, not realizing she is a prostitute, and eventually marries her, much to the amusement of his more worldly friends. Alarcón tells the story of the courtship in an understated way which brings out nicely the irony in the situation. At the same time, the raucous comments of his friends emphasize Rafael's ingenuousness.

"Tic . . . tac" (1875) is a toned-down version of what could have been a bawdy Rabelaisian story. A mistress and her lover are suddenly surprised in her bedroom by the arrival of her husband. When she hides the lover in a wall clock, his body prevents the pendulum from swinging. She tells him her husband cannot sleep if he does not hear the clock ticking, and all night long *tic . . . tac* is heard. The scene shifts to an insane asylum a year later. One of the patients is a young man who continuously clicks his tongue against the roof of his mouth: *tic . . . tac.*

When Alarcón prepared the three volumes of *cuentos* for the edition of the *Obras completas*, he omitted at least three of his previously published stories. Since they deal with love, this seems to be the appropriate place to deal with them. "La cruz de palo" (The Wooden Cross) is dated Guadix, 1852, so it undoubtedly first came out in *El Eco de Occidente* that year, and it was republished in *El Mundo Pintoresco* in 1858.[14] It is a melodramatic love story with a potentially incestuous situation. The action takes place in a feudal castle near Seville in the sixteenth century—the only time Alarcón chose a medieval setting for a piece of fiction. The story calls to mind the extravagant works of the 1830s, and it does not even have verse to cover up its excesses.

Fernando, a troubadour, is in love with Hermenegilda, but her father, Bermudo, the lord of the castle, insists that she marry a wealthy noble to recoup the family fortune. One night while Fernando is serenading Hermenegilda, Bermudo has four of his henchmen waylay the troubadour. Fernando defends himself heroically, killing three of his assailants, but he is finally mortally wounded. Bermudo's brother, a priest, fortuitously arrives and explains that Fernando is Bermudo's son and Hermenegilda's half brother. Bermudo had seduced and then abandoned Fernando's mother, María, a beautiful village girl, and had then abducted their illegitimate child and sent him off to be brought up by his brother in Galicia. María had died soon after, and a villager who had been in love with her erected a wooden cross by her grave on the hillside overlooking the castle. Fernando is buried beside his mother; Hermenegilda enters a convent, and Bermudo becomes insane. The language is as extravagant as the action. Fernando's death is described: "Lying on the girl's skirt, he was passing through the throes of death; the moon shone on his ashen face, beautifying it; he raised his eyes with a painful effort, and upon seeing that angel watching over him during his last hour, there appeared on his rigid lips an ineffable smile of melancholy happiness."[15]

"Dos ángeles caídos" (Two Fallen Angels), one of Alarcón's most implausible stories, first appeared in *El Eco de Occidente* in 1854. It was reprinted in *La Ilustración* in 1855, in *La América* in 1859, and finally in *Cuentos, artículos y novelas*, also in 1859, before being collected in *Dos ángeles caídos y otros escritos olvidados*. After leading a life of debauchery for years, two reprobates miraculously reform and find happiness in marriage. Early in the story the protagonist boasts: "I nourished myself on Byron's bile, Espronceda's disdain, and the frenzy of Jacopo Ortis [an Italian patriot who commits suicide in Foscolo's *The Letters of Jacopo Ortis*]. I despaired of finding a soul worthy of mine, and I swore war on love."[16] We sense that the youthful Alarcón is trying to outdo the most demoniacal writers of the previous generation.

"Mañanas de abril y mayo" (Mornings in April and May), which appeared in *La Ilustración* in 1856 and was collected in the 1866 edition of *Novelas*, is an inconsequential piece about a man who loses the girl he thinks he is in love with to a friend. He misses an early-morning rendezvous with her when he is waylaid by thieves, while the friend courts her in the afternoon and wins her. The early bird does not get the worm. The tone is light, the dialogue frequently clever, and the story ends with a typical Bonnat touch: "Pardon the errors in this story, written on the edge of a printer's tray in a little less than an hour, while a typesetter was leaning over my shoulder to set up the words as they came forth from my pen."[17]

It is understandable why Alarcón omitted these three stories from his *Obras completas*. Yet, "La cruz de palo" and "Dos ángeles caídos," in particular, are of interest because they show him cultivating aspects of Romanticism seldom found elsewhere in his works. "La cruz de palo" resembles a Romantic drama both in setting and plot; while the protagonists of "Dos ángeles caídos," even more than Fabián Conde in *El escándalo*, are extreme cases of satanically Byronic characters fallen into evil, although they, too, finally reform.

III   Narraciones inverosímiles

How is the adjective *inverosímiles* in the title to be interpreted? It is usually translated as "improbable," "unlikely." Montesinos thinks Alarcón chose the title because all the stories, unlike most of those in the other two volumes, are invented, not based on actual events.[18] Alarcón corroborates in the *Historia de mis libros* that almost without exception they were original conceptions, *pura química de mi imaginación* (p. 10).

It is the most heterogeneous of the three collections. It includes two pieces which are not stories at all, the *costumbrista* sketch "Lo que se oye desde una silla del Prado" and "Soy, tengo y quiero" (1854), a dialogue among the author, a writer, and their muse. Two early stories set in northern Norway are in the manner of *El final de Norma*. "El año en Spitzberg" (1855) is no more than an elaboration of the chapter in the novel where Rurico is left to die on the island. "Los ojos negros" (The Black Eyes, 1858) also has an Arctic setting. The Norwegian protagonist plans to take violent revenge on his wife, whose adultery is supposedly proved because she gives birth to a baby with black eyes like her Spanish lover. The situation is the same as in "¿Por qué era rubia?" (Why was she blond?) of *Cuentos amatorios*, although this time it is treated tragically rather than humorously.

"Los seis velos" (The Six Veils), which is dated Paris, 1855, would also seem to fit more appropriately in *Cuentos amatorios*. In the first of the six parts the narrator catches a fleeting glimpse of a young girl looking out the window of a house as he passes through a town in a stagecoach. As the years pass, he happens to see her again as a young mother with her baby, then at a ball being accused by her husband of committing adultery, as a prostitute in a bar, putting flowers on the grave of her child, and finally stretched out in a coffin in a church. Each time the narrator views her through a veil of a different color—white, rose, green, blue, black, and yellow—and the part is titled accordingly. At the end of each episode Alarcón lists a series of objects which the colors symbolize. His vision in brief vignettes of the woman disintegrating from an innocent young girl to an adulteress and prostitute and finally to a corpse is quite in the macabre post-Romantic tradition. At the same time, as Montesinos has pointed out, the extensive use of color symbolism foreshadows Modernism.[19] Alarcón also inserted a number of facetious witticisms a la Bonnat. In the "rose" episode, after enumerating things associated with the color—love, happiness, hope, youth, etc.—he adds: "The color of Quiroga's tooth powder. I recommend it" (p. 234). Actually, the story is so contrived that such waggish interpolations jar less than one might imagine.

The longest of Alarcón's stories, "El amigo de la muerte" (Death's Friend) first came out in *El Eco de Occidente* in 1852, and was subsequently revised and expanded. According to *Historia de mis libros*, the story was originally told to him by his grandmother. He later discovered that the Italian opera *Crispino e la comàre*, which antedates his story by two years, has essentially the same plot. The two authors had independently made use of the same popular tradition. Fernán Caballero's story "Juan Holgado y la muerte" (1850) and Trueba's "Traga aldabas" (1867) also utilize this legend.[20]

Alarcón's story takes place in the early eighteenth century. The sixteen-year-old orphan Gil Gil, supposedly the son of a cobbler, is befriended by the Count of Ríonuevo, who is really his natural father. Gil falls in love with Elena de Monteclara, of a noble family. But when the Count of Ríonuevo dies, his widow casts the boy out. One night, feeling ill and abandoned and despairing of ever winning Elena, he is contemplating suicide, when a mysterious figure who claims to be Death offers to help him. Overnight Gil becomes court physician to Philip V, is able to foretell the death of his son, Louis I, and is rewarded with wealth and a title. The Countess of Ríonuevo suddenly dies, and Gil is free to marry Elena. After the wedding, Death appears and takes him off in a chariot on a fantastic trip around the world, ending in Death's habitat, an icy cavern in the polar region. Six hundred years have passed and it is the year 2316. It turns out that Gil did commit suicide that night in Madrid, and Elena subsequently died of grief. The three days he spent as physician at the court and his marriage to Elena were only something he dreamed after death. Now, his sin of suicide forgiven, he and Elena are united forever in heaven. The first part of the story is recounted in an essentially realistic manner. The historical background and the geographic settings are authentic, although the presence of Death and the prophetic power with which he endows Gil do indeed give a supernatural cast to the story. Then the last part is completely fanciful.

Like "El amigo de la muerte," "La mujer alta" (The Tall Woman), the last story Alarcón wrote, is a supernatural tale with a realistic setting which heightens the feeling of terror. On an excursion in the mountains near the Escorial Gabriel tells the story of his friend Telesforo and his encounters with *la mujer alta* to a group of companions. The first two encounters he describes as Telesforo had recounted them to him. The third, which took place at Telesforo's funeral, had been witnessed by Gabriel himself.

The principal characters, Telesforo, Gabriel, and several of his companions, are engineers, men of science who supposedly would not easily be taken in by the fantastic and the supernatural, and yet they are moved by the story. Alarcón gives specific dates and also precise locations; most of the story takes place in the part of Madrid between the Plaza Santa Ana and the Plaza de las Cortes. In contrast, there is the mysterious and ominous figure of the woman, who seems to have brought on the series of tragedies in Telesforo's life. After the first encounter he discovered that his father had just died. The second time it was his fiancée. The third time it was Gabriel who saw the woman gesticulating at Telesforo's own funeral. Fifteen years have passed since then, and she has not reappeared. Who the woman was, what her relationship with Telesforo was, is never clarified. This mysterious note heightens the effect of the story. When describing her, Alarcón chooses significant details to suggest her maleficent powers and the terror she inspires: her unusual height, her broad and bony shoulders, her owl-like eyes, her protruding nose, the gap in her front teeth which makes her mouth look like a dark hole.

Another late story, "Moros y cristianos" (1881), an amusing tale about hidden treasure, is altogether different from the other *Cuentos inverosímiles*. The five wily individuals in the story double-cross each other. In the end they all die, and no one finds the treasure. The mayor of Aldeire, a small town near Guadix, discovers an Arabic manuscript in the ruins of a Moorish tower on his property. Certain that it contains information about a hidden treasure, he consults a lawyer in a neighboring town. The latter sends the manuscript to his nephew, the choir director of the cathedral of Ceuta in North Africa, asking him to find a trustworthy person to translate it. The nephew consults an Arab appropriately nicknamed Manos Gordas (Fat Hands). He is able to read the manuscript, which does state that a treasure exists but is vague as to its actual location. Realizing that he will be unable to look for the treasure alone, Manos Gordas seeks the aid of a renegade Spaniard who is wanted for murder back in Spain. The renegade kills Manos Gordas and makes his way to Aldeire. Manos Gordas had left a letter with his wife which she was to send to the Spanish authorities if he disappeared, informing them of the renegade's crime. When the latter arrives in Aldeire, he is seized by the police, tried, and executed, but he refuses to divulge anything about the location of the treasure. Shortly afterwards, the mayor, the lawyer, and the nephew in Ceuta all die of natural causes. The treasure, if it existed, lies hidden forever. "Moros y cristianos," with its shrewd popular types, has something in common with "La buenaventura" and "El libro talonario," but this time the characters are too unscrupulous for their own good. The five greedy individuals, each of whom was out to feather his own nest, receive their comeuppance.

As we have seen, there is considerable variety among Alarcón's short stories. He began writing in the post-Romantic period and actually never outgrew these roots, although they are most visible in such early stories as the melodramatic "El clavo," the gruesome "¡Buena pesca!", and even the acclaimed *Historietas nacionales*. His brief "Bonnat" manner, with its emphasis on the facetiously frivolous, illustrates another aspect of this transitional period. The author of *El sombrero de tres picos* also had an excellent sense of the comic, which is evident in such later tales as "El libro talonario" or "La última calaverada." In another vein, the psychologically penetrating "La Comendadora" is an isolated example which stands apart from the rest of his production.

As seen, Alarcón's short stories are not only heterogeneous but uneven in quality. Some of the early ones, understandably enough, date badly, but the best of them hold up well and make up a significant part of his literary production. He was one of the top cultivators of the genre in Spain for three decades, from 1852 to 1882. Otherwise, there were Fernán Caballero, certainly his inferior; Bécquer, whose poetical *leyendas* are very specialized; and Valera, who wrote only a handful of stories during these years. Other lesser lights are pretty much forgotten today.

CHAPTER 4

Cuadros de Costumbres

THE *cuadro de costumbres*, a sketch describing the traditional, popular way of life both in Madrid and in the provinces, was cultivated by most of the writers of the Romantic period. Over fifty of them contributed to the famous 1843 collection *Los españoles pintados por sí mismos*, including Estébanez Calderón, Mesonero Romanos, Zorrilla, the Duque de Rivas, Bretón de los Herreros, Hartzenbusch, García Gutiérrez, and Gil y Carrasco. Of the major Romantic figures, only Larra, who had died, and Espronceda, who wrote little prose, are missing. *Costumbrismo* continued to be popular until the end of the century. The regionalistic note is strong in Fernán Caballero and Pereda, somewhat less so in Valera. Galdós's *Novelas contemporáneas*, most of which are set in Madrid, show the influence of Mesonero Romanos. Palacio Valdés described different regions in his novels, but especially his native Asturias, while Galicia plays an important role in Pardo Bazán's works and Valencia in Blasco Ibáñez's.

I *Autobiographical Sketches*

Regionalism is not a distinctive feature of Alarcón's novels, but he did write a good many *costumbrista* sketches, some based on episodes in his life, others describing scenes he had witnessed in his native Andalusia or in Madrid. In "La Nochebuena del poeta" and "Mis recuerdos de agricultor," as we have seen, he nostalgically evokes his childhood memories of Guadix. The sketches end on a bittersweet note; he is reminiscing about the happy times in a distant past which will never be recaptured. In the delightful "El maestro de antaño" he recalls how much that eccentric but kindly teacher had meant to him.

"Episodios de Nochebuena" is in much the same sentimental vein as "La Nochebuena del poeta," although it does not deal with his

personal experiences.[1] In a series of brief scenes Alarcón describes
how various groups spend the holiday—the obstreperous children
in the working-class district of Maravillas; the people returning from
the Plaza Mayor, laden with provisions; three blind men serenading
a wealthy home; a working-class family, who, full of food and drink,
fall asleep in front of the fire. As Alarcón himself remarks, the sketch
brings to mind Goya and Ramón de la Cruz.

II *Realistic Sketches*

In another group of sketches he describes realistically the life of
the poor and unfortunate both in Madrid and in Andalusia. The tone
is objective, but a note of compassion is present. "El Mundo Nuevo"
is a naturalistic description of the worst slum section of Málaga,
which was ironically called The New World.[2] After detailing the
squalor, the corruption, the lack of familial love, Alarcón concludes
with a reproving admonition: "Málaga, Spain, nineteenth century,
for shame!"

In "Las ferias de Madrid" (The Markets of Madrid) Alarcón
fleshes out a description of a similar district, the *rastro* (flea market)
of Madrid, into a genuine *cuadro de costumbres*.[3] This time he is
more the observant bystander than the moralistic social critic. He
first describes the worthless junk found in the most humble stands
and then progresses to the still useful furniture cast off by those who
have risen in the world. He introduces bits of conversation to lend
variety to his presentation. A washstand says of its former owner
who happens to pass by: "There's my owner! I belonged to him
when he was a clerk. Since he left me, he no longer sings while
washing" (p. 1680). Accumulation and exaggeration are favorite
techniques. He describes the broken and useless objects for sale in
one of the squalid stalls:

One sees all jumbled together half a pair of scissors, half a medal of Isabel
the Catholic, the pedestal from the statue of a saint, used bandages, the tails
of a frock coat, the brim of a hat, a crutch of a cripple who died, a knife
handle, the neck of a guitar, the heel of a boot, a box without a bottom,
three pages from a book, the binding of another, a piece of braid from a
general's uniform, a "widower" shoe, a "bachelor" glove. And everything
dirty, rusty, full of holes, frayed, and plagued, moreover, by the kiss of
death. (p. 1679)

The two adjectives "widower" and "bachelor," applied to cast-off
articles of clothing, lend a humorous touch, likening the odd shoe

and glove to people without mates. In the last phrase the four past participles end in *ado: oxidado, agujereado, deshilachado,* and *apestado;* and the rhyme emphasizes the cacophonous sound of the words. The triteness of the final phrase, *el ósculo de la muerte,* is accentuated by the Latinate word *ósculo.* The description is very much in the tradition of Larra.

There is a similar passage in "El Nuevo Mundo," where he compares that district of Málaga to the *rastro.* Alarcón was obviously pleased with this effort, and since he did not plan to republish the earlier piece, he resolved not to let it go to waste. So, modifying it slightly, he inserted it in "Las ferias de Madrid." This is a practice he frequently followed. Another example is "Granada a vista de buho" (An Owl's View of Granada), which appeared in *El Eco de Occidente* in 1854. In the title he is obviously playing with the expression *a vista de pájaro* (bird's-eye view). In this sketch he evokes a romantically nightmarish vision of Granada at two in the morning, equating night with death. Although it is not one of his more successful efforts, six years later he adapted the sketch, making only minor changes, for *El Museo Universal,* retitling it "Madrid a vista de buho."[4]

In "Verdades de paño pardo" (The Truth about the Ill-dressed) Alarcón presents a naturalistic picture of an impoverished Andalusian family living in squalor and beset by taxes, but the effect is in part spoiled by a long, irrelevant introduction which purports to be humorous but which jars with the serious tone of the body of the sketch. The narrator begins by facetiously listing the various modes of locomotion he has used and admits that he has never ridden on a camel or an elephant. He then says that one spring evening he was traveling in the country on a donkey when it began to storm. Seeking shelter, he saw a light in a peasant's hovel. "I immediately headed the prow of my donkey in that direction, and both the donkey and I began to row with our feet."[5] This far-fetched metaphor does not set the right tone for the ensuing description of the poverty-stricken family. The influence of Karr is already visible in this early piece.

III *The Society Reporter*

Alarcón led an active social life in Madrid in the late 1850s, moving in the most select circles. In 1858 and 1859 he wrote numerous articles for *La Epoca* commenting on the social scene. They are really *cuadros de costumbres,* not mere social notes. Years

later, in 1871, he collected many of these articles, and, after considerable pruning, published them in *Cosas que fueron*. Madrid life
during the various seasons of the year is described in "Diarios de un
madrileño"—the pleasure of taking a stroll in the winter by the
Fuente Castellana which was frequented by elegant women, the
austerity of Holy Week, the revival of activity on Holy Saturday,
and the boredom in the oppressive heat of the summer when
Madrid is virtually deserted. Then, after a holiday in the north, the
fall season is about to get under way again.

In another series, "Visitas a la marquesa," Alarcón purports to
attend the *tertulia* of an imaginary marquesa to gather material for
his weekly column. The tone is light. He pokes fun at his aging
hostess, who has seen fifty Ash Wednesdays go by, although we
later find out she is actually sixty. He suggests that her earlier
conduct had not been exemplary: *De los sesenta . . . que concurren
allí, por lo menos quince han amado a la marquesa en sus años
verdes, o sea en sus verdes años*. (Of the sixty men present, at least
fifteen have loved the marquesa in her youthful years, that is, in her
salad days, p. 1718.) Alarcón cleverly plays with the two figurative
meanings of the color green here. One of the *tertulianos* quips to the
marquesa: "Women are like cheese. Until it begins to spoil, the
connoisseurs don't like it" (p. 1721). In other installments Alarcón
comments on the weather, on a ball given by the Condesa de
Montijo (the mother of the Empress Eugenie), on recent plays; and
he recounts amusing anecdotes about *El Labí* (Manuel Díaz), a
bullfighter who had recently died in Lima. When jeered at by the
French in Bayonne, he is said to have retorted: "I despise you and
all the foreigners here!" (p. 1726).

In these articles Alarcón is describing with amused tolerance the
mostly frivolous pursuits of the wealthy, a way of life he himself
obviously enjoyed. It is seldom that we find him assuming the tone
of the reforming satirist.

IV *Almanac Articles*

During the years following the publication of *Los españoles pintados por sí mismos* in 1843, many imitations of it were brought out.
One of the most impressive was Guijarro's three-volume *Las mujeres españolas, portuguesas y americanas* (1873), to which Valera
contributed the delightful "La cordobesa" and Alarcón the less
successful "La granadina."[6] We shall return to it later. Alarcón

wrote four similar articles for almanacs. The humorous "El año campesino" (The Year in the Country) is the most colorful of the group. He cleverly shows how different social groups divide up time and identify the year an event occurred. Politicians, for example, count by elections, legislatures, and ministries. Alarcón refers to a recurring problem of Spanish bureaucrats, *cesantía*—losing one's job when one's party is out of office:

—During the ministry of Bravo Murillo—one man says—I let my beard grow.
—For heaven's sake! What chance!—says another—That was when I got married.
—What? You were a member of his party?
—I should think so! That's why I got married.
—I let my beard grow because I belonged to the opposition.
—Ah! To show your republican sympathies.
—No, sir. So as not to have to go to the barber's. (p. 171)

In another section he shows how peasants tell people's ages. The popular and colorful language brings out their ingenuousness:

—How old is that young man?
—That one? He must be about to be drafted.
—And the girl?
—The girl? She's getting along. She was born the same day as the lame mule, and the lame mule is dead now.
—And *tía* Ramona?
—*Tía* Ramona stopped bearing children a long time ago. (p. 173)

"Mayo," a trite glorification of that month, appeared in *La Ilustración Española y Americana* in 1877.[7] It begins with a description of the coming of spring, with its plethora of flowers and fruits. Then Alarcón somewhat pedantically lists the names given the month in various ancient civilizations and the important events in Spanish history which occurred during that month. In "Las horas" (The Hours) Alarcón details the various occupations of the Spaniards—the rich and the poor, in Madrid and in the provinces, in summer and in winter, and during the various hours of the day. He manages to make a moderately amusing article out of this rather unpromising idea.[8] "Diciembre" was written for Henrich's luxurious almanac, *Los Meses* (The Months), in 1887.[9] Alarcón had a distinguished group of collaborators, including Valera, Pereda, Campoamor, Castelar, Echegaray, Núñez de Arce, and Galdós. He colorlessly describes December's unpropitious climate and the social activities of the Christmas season. In the final section, "El fin del mundo," he concludes that just as December marks the end of the year, so all moral values in the world have disintegrated and the apocalypse is at hand. This is the last piece Alarcón wrote, and his discouragement and pessimism of those years is strongly reflected in it.

V   *Following in the Footsteps of Larra and*
Mesonero Romanos

Temperamentally, Alarcón and Larra were dissimilar, and their works are different, too. Alarcón did write one political allegory, "El cometa nuevo," which is subtitled "Ensayo astronómico-político," along the lines of Larra's "El hombre globo." Alarcón compares the more than 200 comets which have been observed recently in Spain to the rapid succession of governments during the reign of Isabel II. No one knows where the comets come from or where they are going. In past ages a comet heralded a major event, such as the execution of Alvaro de Luna. Now many of them are seen, but nothing ever happens. The country is in the doldrums. "El cometa nuevo" is a short piece; Alarcón had hit upon a clever conceit, but he did not make the most of its possibilities.

Alarcón certainly had more in common with Mesonero Romanos than with Larra. Two brief sketches show the influence of Mesonero's "Las sillas del Prado" from *Escenas matritenses*. "Lo que se oye desde mi ventana" (1853) consists of a series of brief remarks by passersby supposedly overheard from his window in Granada one night. Some years later he used the same technique in a similarly titled sketch, "Lo que se oye desde una silla del Prado" (What One Hears from a Chair in the Paseo del Prado).[10] This time the fragments are a little longer, giving the author more time to build up his effects. At his best he manages to suggest a situation in a few words. The lack of compassion of the wealthy for the poor:

—Señora! I have three children, and I'm a widow, and I'm sick.
—Heavens! What beggars! They don't let you walk in peace. Excuse me. May God help you.
—Mama, take us to the Café Suizo.
—It's still early. We'll go later.

Two young blades setting out on a spree:

—I? Twenty *cuartos*. And you, how much do you have?
—I? A peseta.
—Then we can go. You will see some real women and do they dance the can-can!

A married woman embarking on an affair:

—Tomorrow, at eight, at St. Sebastian's, in the Virgin's chapel. But be careful. My coachman is beginning to suspect something. (p. 272)

"Cartas a mis muertos," in which Alarcón briefly evokes various dead friends, is in the same vein, although he uses a different technique—the epistolary form rather than over-heard snatches of conversation. His theme is that the dead are quickly forgotten. A widow remarries shortly after her husband's death. The sisters of another friend cease wearing mourning within six months of his death; the following week they are out dancing. Alarcón presents his fickle view of mankind in a light-hearted manner. His satire does not cut deep.

From its title, "Lo que se ve con un anteojo" (What One Sees through a Telescope), first published in *El Eco de Occidente* in 1854, suggests that it is another sketch along the lines of the two *lo que se oye* . . . ones, but it is an altogether different type of work. It is, in fact, one of Alarcón's most deeply felt articles. One day the author was looking through a telescope from the heights of the castle of Gibralfaro in Málaga. After taking in the impressive panorama, he focused on a gathering of people below and discovered that a soldier was about to be executed. He later learned the victim had merely jostled a sergeant during the course of a quarrel over a woman, a misdemeanor for which a civilian would have been punished with five days' detention. Alarcón graphically described the phlegmatic and almost idiotic appearance of the victim. The device of viewing the scene through a telescope heightens the effect. Alarcón was violently opposed to capital punishment, and this sketch has a feeling of passion not often found in his work. "El rey se divierte" (The King Enjoys Himself) treats a similar theme. Extracted from a historical chronicle, *Auto general de fe, celebrado en Madrid en 30 junio de 1660,* it is a description of an auto-da-fé which Charles II witnessed. Alarcón lists the numbers of people burned and their ages without amplification. His revulsion at the barbaric practices of the Inquisition is accentuated here by the laconic, understated approach.

VI   *Fisiologías*

Early in his career Balzac began to cultivate a new type of essay, the *physiologie,* in which he studied certain groups of people or certain professions in an analytical fashion. His best-known work of this type was the early *Physiologie du mariage* (1829). The genre had a huge vogue in France during the next fifteen years. Many of these works were translated into Spanish, and imitations of them began to appear. Larra, Mesonero Romanos, Estébanez Calderón, and Fernán Caballero, among others, were influenced by this new psychological fad.[11] Alarcón published two short pieces of this type, "La fea" (The Ugly Woman) and "La hermosa" (The Beautiful Woman), both in *El Eco de Occidente* in 1854.[12] "La fea" was first subtitled a *costumbre,* then, in subsequent editions, *ensayo fisiológico* and *autopsia.* In this sketch Alarcón divides ugly women into categories, those born homely *(feas naturales)* and those who lost their looks through an accident or an illness such as smallpox *(feas accidentales).* He goes on in this vein until he has created such categories as *fea natural—sin gracia—de la clase media.* It all seems contrived and neither very funny nor enlightening. "La hermosa" is more successful. There is an amusing analytical enumeration in which he plays with the numeral "three":

The perfect beauty must have:

Three white things:	skin, teeth, and hands.
Three black ones:	eyes, eyebrows, and eyelashes.
Three pink ones:	lips, cheeks, and fingernails.
Three long ones:	trunk, hands, and hair.
Three small ones:	teeth, ears, and feet.
Three broad ones:	chest, forehead, and the space between the eyebrows.[13]

Alarcón goes on to satirize the beautiful woman as a heartless coquette. The sketch concludes with a brief dramatic skit. A beauty spurns a poor suitor for a wealthy one. Even after the former commits suicide, the unconcerned beauty continues to be preoccupied only with her looks.

Even such a relatively late sketch as the aforementioned "La granadina" (1873) shows the influence of the *fisiología*. In the first part of the article he calls the titles of the various sections axioms, as: "Todas las granadinas son católicas apostólicas romanas," "La granadina es la señora de su casa" (She is the mistress of her house), "La granadina no cultiva el campo" (She does not work in the fields), etc. The sketch concludes with a diagram listing her supposed attributes and qualities (p. 1179):

Description and Portrait of Her

Person-ality	Moral Char-acter	Clothes	Way of Life	Reli-gio-sity	Beauty	Defects	Inter-ests	Excel-lences
Varia-ble	Exem-plary	Exces-sive	Arab or Pari-sian	Idola-trous	Ideal	None	All	They are begin-ning to be abun-dant in the province

Alarcón's description of his compatriot is rather flat, but the sketch is something of a curiosity, because it shows him anachronistically following techniques which had been popular a generation before.

VII Humorous Sketches

A few miscellaneous sketches are in a humorous vein. "El pañuelo" consists of a series of short scenes ranging in length from a sentence to a page or two in which a handkerchief plays a leading role. Alarcón strives for an antithetical effect by alternating contrasting passages. A scene of romantic young love is sandwiched between a tragic death and a banal incident. The shorter passages are perhaps the most effective because such an artificial device does not hold up well for long: "With it [a handkerchief] a messenger bringing a pardon announces himself at the foot of the gallows./ With it you brush the dust off your boots./ It plays the principal role in Shakespeare's *Othello*" (p. 1684).

In somewhat the same fashion in "Sinfonía. Conjugación del verbo 'amar,' " Alarcón plays with this verb, using different tenses to characterize the speaker: "A fool: I am loved!/ A rich man: I will be loved!/ A poor man: I would be loved!" (p. 30).

Alarcón's production as a writer of *costumbrista* sketches is uneven. The most delightful of them is his evocation of his old teacher, "Un maestro de antaño." Others in which he good-naturedly satirizes the foibles of his contemporaries—"Las ferias de Madrid," "Lo que se oye desde una silla del Prado," and some of his society columns written for *La Epoca*—also hold up well. But, taken as a whole, they do not compare with the best of his fiction. They make up a secondary, if not inconsequential, part of his literary production. What is interesting is that in the 1850s, and even later, Alarcón, the post-Romantic, was still cultivating *fisiologías* and humorous tours de force such as "El pañuelo," which are associated with an earlier era. Unlike his contemporary Pereda, Alarcón sought less to describe the reality he saw around him than to entertain his readers with verbal stunts. "La granadina" is more of a *fisiología* than a *costumbrista* sketch. Similarly, there is rather little *costumbrismo* in his novels. Alarcón was not a regionalist. The aspects of the *cuadro de costumbres* which interested him and which he cultivated most of the time were those which did not fit into the novel. As a result, his sketches and his novels have a limited amount in common.

CHAPTER 5

Travel Pieces

I Articles

ALARCÓN collected five of his travel pieces in *Viajes por España* (Travels Through Spain, 1883), and then added a section, "Recuerdos de mis viajes," listing the many trips he took during the course of his life. In addition to three visits to Paris, his long trip to Italy via Switzerland, and his African expedition, he traveled widely through Spain, on horseback, by stagecoach, and by train. He published accounts of several of these trips in periodicals. The first, "Viaje a París en 1855," a series of six articles on his first trip to Paris primarily to visit the Exposition, came out in *El Occidente* in May and June of that year. Others include "De Madrid a Santander" (1858), with a description of a frightful train accident; "Mi primer viaje a Toledo" (1858), made shortly after the inauguration of rail service between Madrid and Toledo; "El eclipse del sol de 1860," which he witnessed in Sagunto; "Una visita al Monasterio de Yuste" (1873), where Charles V retired after abdicating; and the longest and most interesting of the group, "Dos días en Salamanca" (1878), in which Alarcón describes in some detail the principal monuments of that city.[1] Finally, in 1884, under the title "Más viajes por España," he reminisces about some youthful trips he had taken to Granada, Almería, Málaga, and Cádiz.[2] Spain was just beginning to be linked up by train, and travel was still difficult. So Alarcón's contemporaries must have found what he had to say new, although for today's reader these articles are not terribly interesting, especially when compared with his three major travel books.

II Diario de un testigo de la Guerra de Africa

In the *Diario de un testigo de la Guerra de Africa (1859–1860)* (Diary of a Witness of the African War) Alarcón strove to present a

59

factual account of what he had seen. He did not arrive in Ceuta until December 12, 1859, and so missed the first skirmishes. The Spanish army was slowly fighting its way south along the Mediterranean toward Tetuán under constant attack by the Moors, the biggest engagement being the battle of Castillejos on January 1. The Moors were decisively defeated by the outnumbered Spaniards outside of Tetuán on February 2, and three days later the city fell. The Moroccans sued for peace but refused to meet the Spaniards' demand to give up Tetuán, and the war continued. Alarcón returned to Spain on March 22, the day before the victory of Wad-Ras, which brought about the capitulation of the Moors and the end of the war.

Alarcón is reticent about his own exploits on the battlefield, but we do learn that his foot was severely bruised by a spent bullet in one of the encounters preceding the battle of Castillejos and that he had to be hospitalized in Ceuta. Working closely with the commanding generals, Alarcón was in a good position to see and to evaluate the progress of the war. He was a conscientious reporter, filing almost daily dispatches. He describes the military campaign in a very jingoistic tone, viewing the war as a crusade to avenge the sullied Spanish honor and the Spanish soldiers as heroes. Alarcón was not prejudiced against the Moors, as can be seen in the short sketch "Una conversación en la Alhambra," written a few months earlier, where he shows marked sympathy for their plight after having been banished from Spain. In the *Diario* they are pictured in a more mixed light. At times he vaunts their bravery and their skill as horsemen; at others, he reports that they cravenly flee. Only once, when commenting on their lack of artillery, does he suggest the handicaps under which they are fighting—irregular troops with inferior weapons against trained soldiers. And he does express regret for their suffering. At the same time he never wavers in his belief that the Spanish cause is just. Thus Alarcón at first appears as a superpatriot who justifies and even glorifies the war, but after the capture of Tetuán his attitude is much more compromising. He sees no reason to continue the war and condemns the Spanish for exacting such harsh terms. He obtains his discharge so that he can return to Madrid and work for peace.

The *Diario* is much more than an account of the military campaign. Alarcón describes the often rugged and inhospitable, at times fertile and enticing, African landscape. He tells about how the soldiers live and the hardships they suffer, in particular, the ravages caused by cholera. Actually, over twice as many Spaniards died of cholera as were killed in action. Alarcón stayed for six weeks in Tetuán after its fall. Since little military activity was going on, he spent his time exploring the city and getting to know its Moorish and Jewish inhabitants and their way of life. The Moors come off much better than the Jews, whom he criticizes for being at the same time rapacious and subservient.

Alarcón's nationalistic reports struck a responsive chord in his fellow countrymen. He mentions that he had to burn 20,000 letters from well-wishers when he left Tetuán (p. 14). The press was most eulogistic. A rave review in *La Epoca* by the Valencian poet Teodoro Llorente, heaping praise on Alarcón as a poet, historian, and writer, is typical.[3] With a touch of vanity Alarcón states that 50,000 copies of the book were sold and that the publishers cleared 80,000 *duros* (the *duro* was then worth approximately a dollar). They treated him generously, and henceforth he was comfortably well off.

Although most Spaniards were, like Alarcón, chauvinistic about the war, there were some, including Galdós, who realized that it was an unnecessary intervention which had caused needless bloodshed and suffering. Alarcón appears briefly in *Aita Tettauen*, Galdós's *Episodio nacional* dealing with the African War, which was written in 1904–1905. Shortly before the battle of Castillejos, Juan Santiuste, the protagonist of the novel, spends an evening with Alarcón in his tent. Santiuste chides Alarcón for the luxurious style in which he is living at the front and is openly critical of his reports: "You will put in prose quatrains the slaughter of yesterday and today. You are the only one for this, Perico. It is true that you find the appropriate language to express this epic of Castilian valor and the scorn with which the poor Moors are cruelly viewed. . . . You know how to eliminate the hollow bombast from the martial language, giving it an incomparable elegance."[4] Santiuste, who had formerly supported the war, has become an apostle of peace, and his position reflects Galdós's own nonviolent position.

III   De Madrid a Nápoles

Late in August of that same year (1860), Alarcón set off on his long-awaited trip to Italy. He went by ship from Valencia to Marseilles and then by train to Paris, where he stayed for some six weeks. He devotes only a few pages to describing the city and its monuments, perhaps because he had already done so in his 1855 articles. What is new here is a sharply critical attitude toward the French; Alarcón had become conservative and something of a francophobe. France for him exemplified what was wrong with contemporary civilization. He railed at the paternalistic government of Napoleon III and at the materialistic values with which the French nation had become obsessed. "I asked God, with all the strength of my patriotic ardor, to delay the hour when Spain would become completely civilized, if this civilization is always to produce results like those I had contemplated in France. Because then, and only then, did I fully realize the illness of our century, that is, the cancer which is corroding modern Europe; then, and only then, did I suddenly become converted from a democrat to a conservative, taking fright at the revolutionary spirit which had so captivated me in my earliest youth" (p. 1227).

Alarcón stopped off briefly in Geneva, made an excursion to Chamonix to view Mont Blanc, and eventually entered Italy by stagecoach via the Simplon Pass. He spent three months in that country, taking in the usual sights. After visiting Lake Maggiore and the Piedmont, with its capital Turin, he proceeded east to Milan, Verona, and Venice; then south to Bologna; back to Turin and Genoa; by ship to Pisa and Florence; overland to Rome; and again by ship to Naples, Vesuvius, and Pompeii. In February, he returned to Madrid via Genoa, Turin, Paris, and Bordeaux. Along the way he had the opportunity of meeting three famous people. He spent an evening with his idol, Rossini, in Paris; in Turin he interviewed Cavour; and in Rome he had an audience with the Pope.

The cities and the landscape, particularly Mont Blanc, Venice, and Vesuvius, are described in some detail, but Alarcón concentrates more on the works of art he is seeing for the first time. His evaluations are fairly standard and reveal him as an informed amateur. But this is not the most interesting part of the book for today's reader. Italy was then going through an exciting transitional period in its history. The Austrians still held sway in Venice, but Piedmont, under Victor Emmanuel II, was on the rise, and Garibaldi had taken over Sicily and Naples. The papacy was losing its temporal powers. Alarcón comments on the political situation in the various parts of the country and is particularly critical of the autocratic regime in Venice.

De Madrid a Nápoles came out in two volumes in 1861. Although it was not the huge success that the Diario had been, it was well

received. Upon the occasion of the publication of the second edition
in 1881, Mesonero Romanos wrote very favorably about it—an
interesting sidelight, because this was the only time Mesonero
wrote about Alarcón, even though they had a good deal in common.[5]

IV *La Alpujarra*

La Alpujarra, the southern part of the province of Granada lying
between the Sierra Nevada and the Mediterranean, was until quite
recently one of the most inaccessible regions of Spain. In the
nineteenth century much of it was closed to wheeled traffic. The last
Moorish resistance was centered here. Boabdil withdrew to the
Alpujarra after the fall of Granada in 1492 before crossing over to
Africa, and the Morisco rebellion under Aben Humeya broke out
here in 1578. Alarcón, a native of nearby Guadix, deeply interested
in Spain's Moorish heritage, had long wanted to visit the area.
Finally, in March 1872, his wish was fulfilled, and he spent ten days
traveling through the region. His account of the trip, *La Alpujarra,*
came out two years later. Alarcón and his party set out by stagecoach
from Granada, and, after crossing the valley of Lecrín, they made
the rest of the trip on horseback. They took in the principal towns of
the region, Lanjarón, Orgiva, Albuñol, Murtas, Adra, and then
spent Holy Week visiting towns on the slope of the Sierrra, ending
up in Ugíjar. Alarcón describes the changing countryside, the
magnificent mountain panoramas, the picturesque villages, and the
people he meets; but over half the book is devoted to evoking the
tragic conflict between the Christians and the Moors that led to the
expulsion of the latter. Alarcón draws principally on three histo-
rians, Diego Hurtado de Mendoza, Luis del Mármol Carvajal, and
Ginés Pérez de Hita, quoting from them at length, to recount the
harrowing stories of Boabdil, Aben Humeya, and Aben Aboo. Aben
Humeya rose up against the Christians, but was assassinated in 1579
by his cousin Aben Aboo, who succeeded him to the throne. Aben
Aboo, in turn, was treacherously murdered two years later. The
Moriscos were uprooted and forcibly resettled elsewhere, while
Spaniards from other areas were brought into the Alpujarra to live.
Historical passages alternate with narrative and descriptive ones
throughout the book so the reader is constantly associating the
beautiful country with its calamitous history. The last section is
titled "La Semana Santa [Holy Week] en Sierra Nevada." Each day

Alarcón travels to a new town and describes the manner in which the holy day is celebrated. He quotes at length from the Gospel to reinforce Christ's message of charity and forgiveness. In his *Historia de mis libros* Alarcón states that with a greater display of tolerance the unjust expulsion of the Moriscos could have been avoided and they would gradually have been assimilated by Christian Spain. His tolerance went only so far. Basically a conservative Catholic, he saw no place for Islam in Spain.

CHAPTER 6

Poetry and Drama

I Poetry

A LARCÓN began publishing poems in *El Eco de Occidente* before he was twenty, and he continued writing poetry throughout his life. The collection, *Poesías serias y humorísticas*, appeared
in 1870 with a most encomiastic prologue by Valera. In the third
(1885) edition of this volume, which Alarcón prepared for the "Colección de Escritores Castellanos," he added some new poems,
dropped others, and tacked on the play *El hijo pródigo*. A handful of
late, inconsequential poems came out in *Ultimos escritos* (1891).
Many of his poems remain buried in periodicals and in collections of
one sort or another, but their publication would certainly not affect
our assessment of him as a poet.

As the title suggests, *Poesías serias y humorísticas* is divided into
two parts, although the division is arbitrary, as some of the so-called
"serious" poems are light in tone and many of the "humorous" ones
are, on the contrary, not funny at all. There is considerable variety
in the volume. There are poems, at times almost embarrassingly
sentimental, addressed to his wife and to his daughter Paulina. In an
early ode, "Al océano Atlántico" (1853), he ponderously exalts that
majestic ocean, contrasting it with the placid Mediterranean. He
describes places he visited—Mont-Blanc, Venice, Rome, Vesuvius,
Pompeii. Other poems conventionally sing the praises of a series of
women, some real, some imaginary. He occasionally shows a touch
of irony somewhat reminiscent of Campoamor. These are the poems
which Valera preferred. Among the most successful of them is the
sonnet "El cigarro," with its clever conceit comparing life to a
cigarette.

> ¡Lío tabaco en un papel; agarro
> lumbre, y lo enciendo; arde y a medida

65

que arde, muere; muere, y en seguida
tiro la punta, bárrenla y . . . al carro!
Un alma envuelve Dios en frágil barro
y la enciende en la lumbre de la vida;
chupa el tiempo, y resulta en la partida
un cadáver. El hombre es un cigarro.
    La ceniza que cae es su ventura;
el humo que se eleva, su esperanza;
lo que arderá después . . . su loco anhelo.
    ¡Cigarro tras cigarro el tiempo apura;
colina tras colina al hoyo lanza;
pero el aroma . . . piérdese en el cielo! (p. 310)

(I roll some tobacco in a paper and light it.
It burns, and as it burns, it dies.
It dies, and immediately I throw the butt away.
It is swept away, and off it goes with the refuse.
God wraps a soul in fragile clay
And endows it with the spark of life.
Time puffs away on it and at the end
There remains a cadaver. Man is a cigarette.
The ash which falls is his happiness.
The smoke which rises, his hopes.
What burns afterwards, his mad yearnings.
Time burns up one cigarette after another.
It casts one butt after another into the pit.
But the aroma, it is lost in the sky!)

Rather surprisingly, his poetry has fewer Romantic traits than his prose. In the long historical legend "El suspiro del moro" (The Moor's Sigh), his best-known poem (it won first prize in a contest sponsored by the Liceo of Granada in 1867), he evokes the last Moorish king, Boabdil, his sorrow at losing Granada, and his eventual death in Africa. The poem is descriptive rather than narrative, and the language and the imagery are almost neo-Classical in their inspiration. The bucolic setting is reminiscent of Meléndez Valdés:

También las aves a sus dulces nidos
y a la paz que perdieron retornaban;
los rebaños, ayer despavoridos,
otra vez por las cumbres asomaban;
y cantos, y rumores, y balidos
el aire placidísimo poblaban,
cual si el pasado sanguinoso empeño
hubiera sido imaginario sueño. (p. 281)

(The birds were also returning to their sweet nests
And to the peace which they lost;
The flocks, yesterday terrified,
Were beginning to appear again on the mountains;
And songs and noises and bleatings
Filled the placid air,
As if the past bloody struggle
Had been an imaginary dream.)

Alarcón lacks Zorilla's narrative gift, but at the same time his descriptions do not have the vividness and the color of those of the Duque de Rivas. Boabdil's wife is portrayed by a string of clichés. Her skin is normally the color of a rose, her lips of red carnations. Grief has turned them white like lilies:

> *Mas de su rostro angelical la rosa*
> *y de sus labios los claveles rojos*
> *trocado había pertinaz la pena*
> *en lirio mustio y pálida azucena.* (p. 281)

Valera's uncritical praise of Alarcón's poetry is understandable. He could hardly do otherwise in a prologue for a friend. Pardo Bazán's evaluation is more to the point. Alarcón lacked talent, and she characterized his poetry as *gimnasia de prosista*.[1] The verses quoted above, which are quite typical, read awkwardly with a limping cadence. Missing is the verve found in the best of his prose. "El suspiro del moro" may be his best poem, but it is still a pretty pedestrian effort. Of course, he was writing in a prosaic age. Of his contemporaries, only Bécquer, Rosalía de Castro, and perhaps Campoamor, among the poets, hold up today. Even Valera, certainly a superior writer to Alarcón, was not a success as a poet either.

II   El hijo pródigo

For several years beginning in 1855 Alarcón wrote drama criticism for the Madrid papers. An exacting critic, he treated even established dramatists severely. He understandably found most of what he saw mediocre, and thinking he could do better himself, he decided to give the theater a try. The result was *El hijo pródigo* (The Prodigal Son), a three-act drama in verse, which was still the norm in the 1850s. The subject obviously appealed to him; *El hijo pródigo* was one of the pseudonyms he had used when writing for *El Látigo*.

The play is in part autobiographical. Like Alarcón, Miguel, the protagonist, leaves his native Andalusia to seek his fortune in Madrid. He tries his hand at journalism, becomes involved in politics, and even fights a duel. When threatened by the draft, Alarcón had rushed home. Miguel, after failing in Madrid, also returns to his family.

The entire action takes place in Miguel's family's home in an unnamed Andalusian town. Miguel, in love with a countess (she is married, but her husband is mortally ill), is intent on following her to Madrid and seeking fame as a musician. He pays no attention to his parents' entreaties and spurns Dolores, their ward, who is in love with him. Borrowing money from his friend Fernando, he sets off for Madrid. In the second act we find out that his illusions have been shattered. The countess married someone else after her husband's death, and Miguel is eking out a living playing the piano in a café. Soon the repentant prodigal son returns home. Miguel realizes that he loves Dolores, and the selfless Fernando, who has always loved her and who has just become engaged to her, is willing to bow out of the picture. But Miguel finally recognizes that he has behaved like a cad and does not deserve Dolores. He departs after being blessed by his father, leaving Dolores to Fernando.

This melodramatic, sentimental, essentially humorless play is somewhat akin to the *comédie larmoyante* of the eighteenth century. The characters are all of a piece. The mother, Dolores, and Fernando, who sacrifice everything for the wayward son, are too unselfish to be believable. At the other extreme, Miguel is the complete egotist until his final abrupt change of heart. *El hijo pródigo* expresses a very conservative ideology. A marked change had occurred in the young iconoclastic radical who had written for *El Látigo* only two years earlier. Alarcón censures Miguel for even thinking of leaving home and living his own life in Madrid. Of all his early works, *El hijo pródigo* most strongly shows Alarcón's didactic concerns, which he was to expound in his academy discourse and in *El escándalo* twenty years later.

El hijo pródigo opened on November 5, 1857, and had a modest run of eight or nine performances before closing. For an insignificant work, it stirred up quite a storm in the Madrid press. Almost all the papers reviewed the play, and some even carried summaries of the polemic—who was for and who against. Alarcón's friends had apparently built up the drama glowingly before the premiere. The critics were disappointed with the product, and, remembering Alarcón's own censorial criticism, some of them over-reacted. Of twelve reviews which I found only five were definitely favorable, and they were by friends of his—José Joaquín Villanueva in *El Occidente*, Manuel Fernández y González in *La Discusión* (Alarcón had written for both papers), Ramón de Navarrete in *La Epoca*, G. G. A. (Gertrudis Gómez de Avellaneda?) in *El Estado*, and Nemesio Fernández Cuesta in *El Museo Universal*. The other seven were hostile. Luis Rivera in *Las Cortes* went so far as to damn the work with a disparate collection of epithets: "tiresome, implausible, monotonous, stupid, whining, and prolix."[2] Alarcón had not been well advised to write his play in verse, which he did not handle well, and several reviewers rebuked him for doing so. Juan de la Rosa in *La Iberia* characterized his versification as *trabajosa, violenta y dura* (laborious, violent, and harsh), and both he and Carlos Frontaura in *El Estado* quoted whole series of faulty verses.[3] The author was hurt by what he considered this virulently unjust criticism. He refused to allow *El hijo pródigo* to be played again and then and there gave up writing for the theater. Catalina, his official biographer, claims that the play was really a popular success and that the adverse criticism was the result of a cabal. Be that as it may, *El hijo pródigo*, a colorless little morality play, is a mediocre work, definitely inferior to the best of the stories he was writing during this period.

CHAPTER 7

El final de Norma

IN his *Historia de mis libros* Alarcón states that he first wrote *El final de Norma* in Guadix at the age of seventeen or eighteen, that is, in 1850 or 1851. He had planned a tetralogy, to be titled *Los cuatro puntos cardinales* (The Four Points of the Compass). Upon the completion of *El final de Norma* (north), he began *La madre tierra* (east), but, dissatisfied with his progress, he abandoned the project and burned the embryonic manuscript. Then in 1855, while recovering in Segovia from depression after his humiliating duel with García de Quevedo, he reworked the early version of *El final de Norma*, introducing humorous quips in the manner of Augustín Bonnat. The novel was published that same year both in the *feuilleton* of *El Occidente* and in book form. It was subsequently reprinted in *La Epoca*. Alarcón later purged the novel of most of the stylistic excesses, probably when he revised it for the fourth (1878) edition, and this is the version that has been regularly printed since. Although the first manuscript has been lost, the plot as we know it is no doubt essentially the same. *El final de Norma* is a piece of juvenilia, the melodramatic outpourings of a Romantic imagination. Some years later, in the preface to the fourth edition. Alarcón spoke disparagingly of it: "I wrote *El final de Norma* at a very young age, when I only knew about the world and about men what maps and books had taught me. This novel, therefore, lacks reality and a philosophical basis, body and soul, verisimilitude and transcendence. It is a work of pure imagination, innocent, puerile, fantastic, . . . and, without doubt, more suited for the entertainment of children than for the instruction of adults. . . . To sum up: although I am its father, . . . I am not proud of having written *El final de Norma*" (p. 374). Although Alarcón was assuming a modest pose in this preface, his assessment of the novel was actually all too accurate.

70

I   A *Novel of Intrigue*

In 1850, when *El final de Norma* was first written, Romanticism was far from moribund in Spain. Zorrilla, García Gutiérrez, and Hartzenbusch were all still active. *El final de Norma* is typical of this period. Rather than writing a historical romance in the manner of Walter Scott, Alarcón chose a different form of exoticism, geographical rather than temporal. Whereas for many northern Europeans—Böhl de Faber, the Schlegel brothers, Byron, Gautier, Hugo, Mérimée—Spain was the romantic country par excellence, Alarcón chose the Arctic wastes of northern Norway and Spitzbergen for his setting. At that time Europeans were beginning to become interested in the polar region, to make journeys of exploration, and to write about it in popular journals. The youthful Alarcón was attracted to this little-known and mysterious part of the world. As we have already seen, he also used it as a setting for two short stories, "El año en Spitzberg" and "Los ojos negros." His knowledge of that distant region was certainly scanty. The only place he describes at any length is the Norwegian town of Hammerfest, with its canals, sheltered port, and cafés, where the inhabitants spend the interminable winter nights drinking. The other details are perfunctory—the snow-covered hills, the icebergs floating by, the herds of reindeer, the various Arctic birds. Thus the setting of the novel is so summarily sketched in that the local color is not particularly effective.

It is the rapid-moving, melodramatic plot which carries the reader's interest. *El final de Norma* is a love story, but, unlike typical Romantic works, it ends with the two pairs of lovers happily getting married. The action is seen through the eyes of the protagonist, Serafín and, to a lesser extent, those of his friend Alberto. They do not know what is going on, who the beautiful soprano and her strange companions are, or what the relationship is among them, and the reader, therefore, is also kept in the dark. The mystery is maintained almost to the end of the novel, when the identity of Brunilda is revealed and the confusion between Rurico and Oscar resolved.

The novel is divided into four parts, followed by a brief epilogue. The first section, "La hija del cielo" (The daughter of heaven), the romantic epithet Serafín gives Brunilda, is the most convincing, largely because the action takes place in Cádiz and Seville, and the setting rings true. Serafín meets his friend Alberto by chance in

Seville, where the former has come to see his sister, Matilde. Alberto is interested in her, but Serafín, wary of his friend's Don Juan tendencies, tells him his sister is married. When Alberto later discovers this to be a falsehood, surprisingly enough he does not hold it against Serafín. He describes to Serafín the beautiful blond foreigner who is singing in Bellini's *Norma* that night, and Serafín is intrigued. A talented violinist, he persuades the conductor to allow him to take his place, and he both conducts the orchestra and plays the violin. The two of them perform magnificently and, in the process, fall in love. Alarcón synthesizes their growing love with the dramatic tension of the opera. At the end, the emotional Serafín even bursts into tears. One wonders how they managed to keep control over their art. Flaubert (Emma Bovary at a performance of *Lucia di Lammermoor*) and Clarín (La Regenta at *Don Juan Tenorio*) use this device in a more convincing manner, for their protagonists are mere spectators, not actual performers. Numerous times during the course of the novel Alarcón returns to this musical theme: Serafín hears Brunilda singing the finale from *Norma* on board ship; when in Hammerfest they are about to part forever, they perform it together.

Brunilda is accompanied by two mysterious Nordic men, one tall, young, and sinister-looking, the other shorter and older. Serafín and Alberto follow her to Cádiz. Serafín is scheduled to make a long-awaited trip to Italy; Alberto, to the polar regions. But there is a mix-up in the tickets, and, while under the influence of alcohol, they board the wrong ships.

The second part of the novel, "Rurico de Cálix," takes place on the ocean and ends with their arrival in Hammerfest. Upon awakening the next day, Serafín discovers his mistake. He also learns that the captain of the ship is the ominous Nordic, supposedly named Rurico de Cálix, and that Brunilda is also on board. The novel is two-thirds over, and the reader still does not know who Rurico and Brunilda are and what the relationship is between them.

The mystery finally starts to unravel in the brief third section, "Historia de Brunilda." In Hammerfest, just before they are to part forever, Brunilda tells Serafín the story of her life. She was born in the nearby castle of Silla, where she spent an isolated childhood. Her tutor, almost her only companion, had developed her great musical talent. One summer, two men, a blond flutist and a dark-haired harpist, roamed around the castle, courting her from a distance. Suddenly, the blond, Oscar *el encubierto* (disguised), seized her father and was about to kill him, when the harpist, Rurico de Cálix, rushed up and, shooting Oscar, saved his life. As reward, he asked for her hand in marriage, and her father readily acquiesced. Subsequently, Oscar, who had only been wounded, pursued Rurico to Spitzbergen and wounded him mortally. Oscar then returned, killed her father, and assuming the identity of Rurico, came to claim her. She requested and obtained a delay of four years, asserting she needed to know him better before marrying him. During these years they had traveled together with the other Nordic, her uncle and guardian, and she had sung in the principal capitals of the world. Now the four years are almost up. In two months she is to marry the supposed Rurico in Silla. She is still ignorant of his true identity and does not know that it was he who murdered her father, but now Serafín has finally found out who *she* is.

The fourth part of the novel is titled "Spitzberg," although only one chapter takes place in that inhospitable archipelago. After Brunilda's departure, Serafín falls sick in Hammerfest and remains unconscious for a month. When he recovers, Alberto providentially reappears, the owner of a ship, the *Matilde,* in which he has been exploring the polar region. In Spitzbergen he had discovered the corpse of Rurico embalmed in the ice with the memoirs he had managed to write before dying. The imbroglio has finally been cleared up. Serafín now knows the identity of his rival and the two murders he has committed. They race madly to Silla and arrive just as the wedding ceremony is about to begin. When Alberto accuses Oscar of being an impostor, the latter challenges him to prove it. He is unable to do so because Rurico's body cannot be retrieved from Spitzbergen until the following summer. Alberto and Serafín vacillate. It appears that Serafín is going to lose Brunilda after all, when Rurico's insane mother appears, hysterically declaims that Oscar is not her son, stabs him, and falls dead over his body. Now Serafín is free to marry Brunilda, and, convinced that Alberto has outgrown his philandering propensities, he no longer puts obstacles in the path of his friend's marrying Matilde.

By not disclosing the identity of Brunilda and Oscar until the last part of the novel, Alarcón builds up suspense. The melodramatic incidents—the confusion in ships, Oscar's palming himself off as Rurico, Alberto's fortuitous arrival in Hammerfest, the opportune appearance of Rurico's mother—whet the reader's interest even though they strain his credulity. One can see how· an ingenuous reader, particularly in the past century, would be caught up in the story, even though today we can scarcely take it seriously.

Our novelist set out to tell a fanciful and melodramatic tale. Plausibility and verisimilitude were of little concern to him. He paid scant attention to the setting, and his characters are not studied in any depth. During the performance of *Norma* Serafín falls hopelessly in love with a woman he has never even spoken to. He is captivated by her beauty, her talent, and by the mysterious aura surrounding her. Yet he is an indecisive hero, slow to act, somewhat like the Duque de Rivas's Don Alvaro. He claims to be unable to live without her. Yet he acquiesces to her marrying a man she loathes, considering her vows to be inviolate. Then, in the climactic scene, Serafín is about to bow out, even though he knows his adversary is an impostor, until Rurico's mother saves the situation. Brunilda is likewise a shadowy, ill-defined character, and she plays a passive role in the novel.

Oscar, Serafín's antagonist, is of a different kind. He, too, loves Brunilda, but, unlike Serafín, he will go to any extreme to win her. He kills both her father and his rival, Rurico, and then assumes the identity of the latter. Serafín's friend Alberto serves mainly as a catalyst to the action. It is he who first kindles Serafín's interest in Brunilda and who finds Rurico's body embalmed in the ice and thus exposes Oscar's treachery and Machiavellian change of identity. In the first part of the novel he is described as a Don Juan type, like Fabián Conde in *El escándalo*, although we never see him in action in this capacity.

II *Style*

Alarcón's style in *El final de Norma* is of a piece with the plot; the exaggerative language reinforces the melodramatic quality of the action. He tends to fall into Romantic excesses, particularly in the serious moments. In the opening chapter, while approaching Seville on board ship, Serafín describes the evening with inflated bombast: "Nature displayed that lethargic tranquillity which comes after serene and resplendent days, as sleep, the younger brother of infallible death, always follows the happy periods of our life" (p. 375). The pretentious metaphor comparing sleep to death rings completely false. He describes Brunilda singing *Norma* by stringing together a series of banal metaphors. Her hair is compared to a rain of gold, her forehead to mother-of-pearl, her eyes to the blue Andalusian sky, her cheeks to snow, and her teeth to tiny drops [*sic*] of ice. Subtlety of language is lacking in *El final de Norma*. In his later fiction Alarcón rids himself of the most obvious exaggerations of this youthful intemperance.

Alarcón did make an effort to use innovative techniques which were not common then. Chapter VI of Part II, "Serafín reflexiona," begins with a series of thirty-four brief interior monologues. One evening on board ship, he meditates on his situation, his adversary, and the woman he loves, and punctuates each monologue with a final exclamation. The execution is less successful than the original idea, for the comments tend to be superficial and obvious: "Who is she? I don't know./ He loves her. Bad!/ She loathes him. Magnificent!" (p. 405).

Another chapter of an experimental nature was extensively altered in the final version of the novel. In the 1855 edition, the second chapter, "Presentación," was written as a dialogue among the author, the reader, and the traveler (Serafín). On the voyage from Cádiz to Seville the author introduces the reader to Serafín; afterwards, the two of them comment briefly about the musician. It was a novel idea, although the dialogue is flat and pedestrian. The later version of the chapter is much superior. It still consists largely of conversation with several of the ship's passengers again giving their impressions of Serafín, but Alarcón no longer uses the typographical form of a play.

The early edition of *El final de Norma* is one of the best places to study Alarcón's early "Bonnat" manner.[1] Following in the steps of his friend, Alarcón makes a show of treating even serious subjects in a burlesque fashion. He addresses the reader directly, treats him ironically, plays him down. He inserts digressions, often preposterously facetious, occasionally lyrical in tone. He cultivates exaggerated metaphors in the manner of Gómez de la Serna's *greguerías*. He uses unconventional typography: chapters only a sentence or a phrase long, many short paragraphs and sentences, frequent ellipses. The reader is constantly being startled by these incongruous stunts, which jar with the Romantic tone of the novel.

When Alarcón revised *El final de Norma*, he did not delete all the "Bonnat" passages. A few either escaped his attention, or perhaps they were purposely retained. Early in the novel, when Serafín and Alberto first meet in Seville, the former rhapsodizes about the trip to Italy which he is about to undertake. His friend makes fun of his effervescence: "This peninsula—interrupted Alberto, parodying Serafín's ardor—this peninsula made by a shoemaker is, according to a certain geographer, giving Sicily a kick in order to send it over to Africa!" (p. 378). The description of the performance of *Norma* ends on a prosaic note which jars with the tone of the preceding chapters: "And the curtain fell, as is the custom in all the theaters in the world" (p. 385). With these ironic touches which break the mood of the novel Alarcón seems to be deriding its Romantic excesses.

The 1855 edition also contained a so-called prologue in five parts scattered through the novel which was later eliminated. In the first section, which served as an introduction, he described the genesis of the novel. He conceived the original idea of the tetralogy one night on the beach in Cádiz when he was nineteen, and *El final de Norma* is now giving body to this youthful dream. This account differs somewhat from what he had to say some years later in *Historia de mis libros*. After Chapter Three, under the rubric "The Prologue Continues," there is a single sentence: "But with all this, *señora*, I forgot to dedicate this novel to you." The reader is referred to a footnote: "Who can this *señora* be? (Note by the reader)."

At the beginning of Part IV, another installment of the supposed prologue contains a long and facetious disquisition on Alarcón's vocation as a writer. He concludes asserting that he is different from other contemporary authors:

> I don't speak to the *masses*, like Sue.
> Nor do I wither the soul, like Balzac.
> Nor do I cause horror, like Soulié.
> Nor do I have bad intentions, like Karr.
> Nor the bad taste to be such a good novelist as Walter Scott.
> Nor am I a poet with talent like Chateaubriand.
> Nor do I glorify *the ugly*, like Victor Hugo.
> Nor do I make people weep, like Lamartine.
> Nor make them bite like Jules Janin.
> Nor am I as pornographic as Paul de Kock.
> Nor as good a poet as Fenimore Cooper.
> Nor as much of an atheist as Pigault Lebrun.
> Nor as skeptical as George Sand.
> Nor as English as Dickens.
> Nor as extravagant as Alfred de Musset.

Nor as much of a dandy as Charles Nodier.
Nor do I lie as much as Alexander Dumas, senior.
Nor do I tell the truth as often as Alexander Dumas, son.

This list was calculated to discourage critics from comparing him to established and famous writers. It was a light-hearted and cute defensive tactic to keep his work impervious to irony. He uses here several of his favorite devices to achieve a humorous effect—accumulation, parallel construction, and antithesis, as in his comments on Scott and the two Dumas. His one-line characterizations of the various writers range from the deliberately superficial to the ridiculous.

Alarcón also eliminated from the 1855 edition certain other chapters which were irrelevant to the main story. Many of them, often only a few lines long, are humorous in tone, as though Alarcón were making fun of his own technique and putting the reader off. In Part IV, Alarcón inserted a chapter numbered 0, and in a footnote said that since the chapter had been lost, he had numbered it zero. He began by quoting as epigraph a quatrain by Espronceda from "El estudiante de Salamanca" about the pleasures of life which have disappeared. Then the text proper of the chapter consisted of seven rows of dots. Alarcón saved this identical device for his later contribution, "Las ruinas del sombrero" (The Ruins of the Hat), to the collection of humorous sketches called *El sombrero*.[2]

A number of amusing topical quips were struck from the final version; they, too, jarred in context. For example, the chapter (Part IV, Chapter IV) in which Serafín learns from Alberto that the supposed Rurico is an impostor and Brunilda is therefore free to marry him was first titled "How Our Hero First Subscribed to *La Esperanza* [Hope]." *La Esperanza* was a conservative Catholic newspaper in Madrid. Alarcón later changed the title to "Reverdece la esperanza" (Hope Comes to Life Again), eliminating the outrageous pun.

The "Bonnat" passages were in large part a defensive mechanism by a young author who lacked confidence and who felt the need to insert some "smart stuff" to avoid being laughed at for the wrong reasons. Most of them strike us today as rather amusing, especially since we do not take the novel as seriously as the nineteenth-century reader did. Alarcón obviously felt in time that the outrageous quips and digressions were puerile and a distracting influence, so he removed the majority of them.

Alarcòn was twenty-two when *El final de Norma* came out in 1855. At that point he had published only a few short pieces and was virtually unknown. As was to be expected, the novel passed unnoticed by the critics, but it was apparently well received by the public. It was reprinted in three other periodicals, and subsequent editions continued to appear. As partial explanation for the popularity of a mediocre and implausible book, it can be said that this was a bleak period in Spain, particularly as far as the novel is concerned, and that *El final de Norma* compares not unfavorably with its competition. It even found approval abroad and was translated into French (1866), English (1891), and Magyar (1906). It continues to be read today; twenty-two editions of it have been brought out in the "Colección de Escritores Castellanos." The critics, understandably, have devoted little attention to it; for them, it is of historical interest as an example of Alarcón's early Romantic manner. Montesinos with reason said of it that "its artistic merits are very inferior to those of the majority of the short stories which Alarcón wrote during those years," and he went so far as to use the adjective *hilarante* to characterize it.[3] The public obviously reacted differently. Instead of being turned off by the sketchy setting and the stereotyped characters, it was caught up by the extravagant plot.

CHAPTER 8

El sombrero de tres picos

IN the preface to *El sombrero de tres picos* Alarcón says that as a boy he first heard the *romance* "El Corregidor y la Molinera" (The Corregidor and the Miller's Wife) recited by a shepherd, *tío* Repela. Subsequently he had been present when other, more scabrous versions had been recounted by village wags, and he had encountered the tale in the famous *Romancero* of Agustín Durán (1849) and in chapbooks as well. Realizing its potential, he suggested it as a possible theme to his friend José Joaquín Villanueva, who began a *zarzuela* entitled "El que se fue a Sevilla" but died before finishing it. Alarcón then recommended it to Zorrilla as the subject for a play, but when, after some time, the later had not even got started, Alarcón took back his idea and made use of it himself for his most famous novel.[1]

In the *Historia de mis libros* written ten years later Alarcón gives quite a different version of the genesis of the novel. In the summer of 1874, having been commissioned to write a comic tale for a Cuban journal, he thought of "El Corregidor y la Molinera" and quickly tossed off a short prose version of it. Then, realizing that he was not taking full advantage of the subject, he began to expand it. A friend to whom he read the first installment was enthusiastic and urged him to publish it in Spain rather then sending it to Cuba. He set to work and six days later *El sombrero de tres picos* was finished. It came out in the *Revista Europea* between August 2 and September 6, 1874, and in volume form the following month (pp. 19–20).

The story of *El sombrero de tes picos* is so well known that it scarcely requires retelling. Lucas, a miller, and his beautiful wife Frasquita live on the outskirts of a small Andalusian city. There, every afternoon, come the bishop, other clerics, and the town authorities, including the lecherous corregidor (the chief magistrate of the city), to partake of the simple hospitality and to admire the miller's wife. When the corregidor arrives early one afternoon and finds her supposedly alone, she repulses his advances and makes a fool of him. Vowing revenge, with the aid of his *alguacil* (bailiff), Garduña, he lays plans to seduce Frasquita that night and orders Lucas to report to the mayor of a neighboring village. But the ill-favored seductor falls into the millrace. Frasquita, taking pity on him, lets him into the house to dry off but then takes off to find her husband. Meanwhile, Lucas, who immediately saw through the corregidor's machinations, returns to the mill. Looking through the keyhole of the bedroom door, he sees the corregidor, who, half-frozen, has climbed into his bed. Although he cannot see her, he assumes Frasquita is there beside him. Lucas first considers killing the corregidor but rejects the plan, for he would only be condemned by the law and hanged. He then resolves to take revenge in kind, and, putting on the corregidor's clothes, sets out for the city. Frasquita, discovering that Lucas has escaped, returns to the mill with Garduña and the mayor. Finding the corregidor now dressed in the miller's clothes, they realize what Lucas has in mind and hurry to the city. There, in a confrontation of the principal characters, the situation is resolved. The millers, convinced of each other's innocence, are readily reconciled. The virtuous corregidora has not been fooled by Lucas's hoax, and, disgusted by her husband's behavior, she banishes him from her bedroom for life. The novel ends with the complete discomfiture of the unprincipled corregidor.

I *Sources*

The antecedents and sources of the novel have continued to intrigue scholars. The first was Menéndez y Pelayo's disciple Bonilla y San Martín who proposed in 1905 three antecedents: the eighth tale from the eighth day of the *Decameron;* the ballad "El Molinero de Arcos" from Durán's *Romancero general;* and a *canción* from a *pliego de cordel* (a song printed on a broadside), "El Corregidor y la Molinera."[2] Boccaccio's tale differs markedly from the other versions and can scarcely be considered an antecedent. A man finds that his best friend is having relations with his wife. He makes the wife shut her lover in a chest, and then seduces the lover's own wife. After this, the four of them dine together and they subsequently become a *ménage à quatre*. It is a tale of double adultery, but the two men are friends and belong to the same social class, whereas in the other versions an influential aristocrat seduces, or tries to seduce, the wife of a man of humble station.

The ballad from Durán's *Romancero*, "El Molinero de Arcos," the work of one Pedro Marín, differs little from the other nineteenth-century versions. The protagonist is now a miller, although his adversary is a *depositario*, a public treasurer, not a *corregidor*. He uses a stratagem to get rid of the miller so he can seduce his wife, who, incidentally, is not averse to the plan. The miller, returning earlier than expected, finds the two of them asleep in bed. He exchanges clothes with the *depositario* and proceeds to the latter's house where the servant mistakenly takes him for the master and lets him in. The miller gains revenge, in turn seducing the *depositario*'s wife. The next morning the four of them celebrate the consummation of the double adultery with a sumptuous breakfast. Bonilla's third item, the song, tells essentially the same story, although now the *depositario* has become a *corregidor*.

Three years later, the French scholar Foulché-Delbosc published two other versions of the song, dated 1821 and 1859.[3] These differ from Bonilla's mainly by the addition of a particularly bawdy stanza recounting the corregidora's surprise at the miller's passionate lovemaking. Foulché-Delbosc also reprinted an 1862 *sainete* (a one-act farce), likewise entitled "El Corregidor y la Molinera," with further variations. The anonymous author has added two characters, Blas, the miller's brother and confidant, and an *alguacil*, the forerunner of Alarcón's Garduña. In addition, the corregidor's three-cornered hat appears for the first time. Basing himself on the lines spoken by the miller at the end of the work,

> The vengeance has been equal:
> You dined with Teresa,
> And I with your wife.
> We'll leave it to the curious reader to decide
> If something untoward occurred after the meal,

Foulché-Delbosc postulates that the *sainete* may have been Repela's relatively chaste version, since the author does not specify that either case of adultery actually took place. But this seems dubious, for a close reading of the text suggests that at least the corregidor was successful in his adulterous quest.

In 1928 the American Joseph Gillet reprinted yet another version of the ballad with minor differences from Durán's. It probably first came out between 1790 and 1823 and is thus the earliest of the Spanish sources so far encountered.[4]

In recent years scholars have turned up variations of the story in several Western European languages. Edwin Place cites a medieval French work, *La Farce du Poulier*, in which a miller significantly named Lucas foils the lascivious designs of two gentlemen to seduce his wife, tricking them, locking them in the hen coop, and then seducing their wives. In this version the miller's wife maintains her virtue.[5] J. A. van Praag summarizes a Dutch work, *Farce of the Shoemaker, or like Monks, like Cowls*, first published in 1660, which follows the same general plot line as the nineteenth-century Spanish versions, although the protagonist is a shoemaker rather than a miller.[6] Armistead and Silverman have recently found more European variants: A German ballad of the sixteenth century, "A Beautiful Amusing New Song, to Read and to Sing, about a Noble and a Shoemaker, Which Took Place in the Town of Krembs," and a Danish ballad, "Cobbler and Nobleman," of the following century.[7] Van Praag's Dutch farce differs in details from the earlier Danish and German ballads, but it clearly derives from the same pattern. Alarcón was, of course, unaware of these early, obscure works, but they make it evident that the tale formed part of the Western European folkloric tradition.

II   *Theme*

In addition to the Durán ballad "El Molinero de Arcos," Alarcón was almost certainly acquainted with some version of the song "El Corregidor y la Molinera," reprinted by Bonilla and Foulché-Delbosc, and probably with the farce published by the latter. In spite of differences in detail, these works have much in common—they are all short, bawdy, and they view love (and sex) with an irreverent eye. Alarcón says that *tío* Repela's version, the one he is going to follow, was much less broad than others he had heard and did not end with the double case of adultery. Some such version may turn up one day. On the other hand, Alarcón may simply have changed the story to suit his own purpose.

The comic effect of the early salacious versions lies almost exclusively in the miller's adulterous revenge and the ironic reconciliation afterwards. In Spain adultery can be treated humorously only in such ribald, extraliterary works. Otherwise, it is dealt with seriously, tragically, as by Calderón. When the younger Dumas wrote Alarcón reproaching him for not having kept the scabrous ending, Alarcón indignantly rejected the criticism (p. 20). Broad farces such as Feydeau's *vaudevilles* were possible in France, not in Spain.[8]

Alarcón altered his characters to fit the change in theme. In the earlier Spanish versions the miller's wife had been a more than willing partner in transgression. Alarcón's Frasquita zealously defends her virtue. The corregidor is no match for her. Here the traditionally vigorous Don Juan has become a devious, decrepit, and lecherous old man. In the early part of the novel Lucas is the devoted husband with complete confidence in his wife. Yet Alarcón claims the miller possessed the traditional Spanish concept of honor: "Lucas was in every point a man, a man like one of Shakespeare's, of few but strong emotions, incapable of doubt; a man who must trust or die, love or slay; who admitted no degrees or middle paths between supreme felicity and the total extinction of happiness." But then Alarcón slyly destroys the effect: "He was, in fine, a Murcian Othello in rope-sandals and a peasant's cap [*con alpargatas y montera*], in the first act of a possible tragedy" (p. 449). It seems unlikely that an Othello would come from Murcia, perhaps the least romantic of Spanish provinces, nor could he wear *alpargatas* and a *montera*. Finally, the word "possible" makes us realize that the novel will end happily. Later, when Lucas thinks Frasquita has betrayed him, he rejects the traditional bloody revenge: "The one difference was that by temperament Lucas was less tragic, less austere, and more of an egoist than the mad slayer of Desdemona" (p. 464). Lucas reacts rationally, not emotionally. He reasons that if he behaves in the customary fashion and kills the corregidor, he will end up hanging. So he will take his revenge another way, as in the earlier versions of the story. The phrase he utters, as he sets out for the city, "the corregidora is beautiful, too," obliquely suggests his plan. We sense, however, that he is not going to be successful, and when we later meet the corregidora, as austere and stalwart in her virtue as Frasquita, we realize why.

Although *El sombrero de tres picos* is a short novel, Alarcón had more room to work with than the anonymous authors of the earlier versions. He fleshed out his principal characters and added new ones. Garduña, who as the *alguacil* had played a minor part in Foulché-Delbosc's *sainete*, is now the corregidor's insidious shadow and lieutenant. The corrupt and ignorant mayor, Juan López, and his aide, Toñuelo, are fitting accomplices. The bishop and the other members of the *tertulia* lend a picturesque, yet, at the same time, unrealistic note to the novel. In the conservative Spanish society of that era we cannot imagine them being intimates of the miller. Alarcón thus broadened the spectrum of the humor so that it does not depend almost entirely on an off-color situation. As a consequence, he created a delightful comic novel, the definitive treatment of the theme of the miller and the corregidor.

III   *Setting*

The setting of the earlier Spanish versions varies among Arcos, Jérez de la Frontera, or some other unnamed Andalusian town. Alarcón simply tells us that his story takes place in Andalusia, but, although he does not name the town, it is patently Guadix. His friend Manuel de Góngora identified some of the places mentioned in the novel and hypothetically associated certain of the characters, in particular the corregidor and Garduña, with historical figures.[9] Although progress had passed Guadix by, leaving it in stagnant isolation, Alarcón felt a nostalgic attachment to his native town, and this comes through in the novel. The time is left indeterminate, sometime between 1804 and 1808, just prior to the French invasion. Napoleon is here portrayed as a remote and almost legendary figure, who had not yet transformed Spanish life.

Life in Spain then is pictured as superficially tranquil and idyllic, and Alarcón even purports to regret his youthful liberal ideals, which had contributed to discrediting the old traditional way of life. He interrupts his description of the corregidor to philosophize:

There are people, not a few, still surviving who could speak out of a full knowledge of that scarlet cape and the three-cornered hat. Ourselves, among the number, as well as all those born in that city during the last days of the reign of Don Fernando VII, can remember to have seen hanging from a nail, the unique adornment of a dismantled wall in the ruined tower of the house once occupied by his Lordship (a tower given over at this time to the innocent games of his grandchildren), those two antiquated articles of apparel, the cape and the hat—the black hat on top, the red cape beneath— forming a kind of specter of absolutism, a sort of winding-sheet of the corregidor, a kind of retrospective caricature of his authority, drawn in charcoal and ochre, like so many others, for us little Constitutionalists of 1837, who were in the habit of meeting there; in short, a kind of *scare-crow*, which in other days had acted as a *scare-man*, and which still frightens me today when I recall that I myself helped to jeer at the thing, carried in the procession through that historic city in Carnival time, tied to a chimney sweep's broom, or serving as a comic disguise for the idiot who could best make the crowd laugh. Poor principle of authority! This is the pass to which we have brought you, we who are never tired of invoking you today! (pp. 449–50)

El sombrero de tres picos does not, however, show Alarcón in such a reactionary light as the above quotation suggests. In retrospect the times may have been picturesque, but they had also been unprogressive, and corruption and injustice had been omnipresent: "Happy times," comments Alarcón, "in which our land enjoyed quiet and peaceful possession of all the cobwebs, all the dust, moths, all the observances, beliefs, traditions, all the uses and abuses sanctified by the centuries!" (p. 445). The corregidor is not only a lecher but is without principles. The sycophantic Garduña, Juan López, and Toñuelo are his henchmen. The illiterate Juan López, unable to make a *rúbrica* (the flourish at the end of a signature which Spaniards use instead of their initials), signs the letter which the corregidor has had written for him with an X.[10] The first edition had *firma* (signature), which Alarcón later felicitously changed to *rúbrica*.[11] After revealing that Juan López had stolen from the *pósito pío*, a charitable storehold which lent grain to widows and poor farmers, Garduña characterizes him as a gambler and a drunkard, always chasing skirts, the scandal of the village, and then concludes: "And that man's a person in authority. That's the way the world goes" (pp. 457–58). Garduña, as big a rascal as Juan López, has little cause for self-righteousness. The chapter is significantly entitled "Le dijo el grajo al cuervo" (Said the Jackdaw to the Crow, or the pot called the kettle black). In addition to Garduña, Alarcón is also referring to the *tertulianos*, who, on the way home, accuse each other of being in love with Frasquita.

Alarcón portrays the backwardness of the country and the all too prevalent abuses in an ironical tone suggestive of Valera. Life was easy for the well-to-do. We are told that at two o'clock of an October afternoon the important people of the town had eaten and were preparing to take their daily siesta, especially those who by reason of their position (the town authorities) had spent the *whole* morning working. Communications were so chaotic that people scarcely knew what was going on in the world: "Once a week (twice at best) the mail from Madrid arrived in most of the important towns of the peninsula, bringing a few copies of the *Gaceta* (which was not, any more than the mail, a daily event), and from it the select few learned (supposing that the *Gaceta* happened to mention it) whether there was a state less beyond the Pyrenees, or another battle had been fought in which six or eight kings and emperors had taken part, or whether Napoleon happened to be in Milan, Brussels, or Warsaw" (p. 445). The people lived "wrapped up in their moth-eaten habits . . . with their picturesque inequality before the law." Alarcón enumerates twelve different forms of taxation imposed on the people, and adds that there were fifty more "whose nomenclature is not now to the point" (p. 445). Accumulation is a comic device which Alarcón uses repeatedly and effectively. Shortly afterwards, he lists fourteen examples of the various favors Lucas asked for and received in exchange for entertaining the authorities at his daily *tertulia*, going so far as to include one hardly in keeping with the miller's character: "Today I gave a man a thrashing and I think he ought to go to jail for having picked a fight with me" (p. 446). Alarcón tells us that the *tertulianos* that evening "made their way toward their respective homes, guiding themselves by the stars like navigators or groping round corners like blind men, since the night had already closed in, the moon had not yet risen, and the public lighting (like the other lights of this century) existed only in the divine mind" (p. 456). His irony lends a humor and charm to *El sombrero de tres picos* which are seldom found in his longer, more ponderous novels. Alarcón's ambivalent feelings about Spain's quaint past with all its discomforts and injustices are nicely summed up in the above-quoted phrase "picturesque inequality before the law."

IV *Characters*

After the preliminary chapters giving the setting, Alarcón introduces his three principal characters, devoting a chapter to each. In the first, "A Woman Seen from Without," he begins by describing Frasquita's charm and beauty which have captivated all the members of the *tertulia*, particularly the corregidor. He then brings out her comic side: she is uncommonly large, taller than her husband, stronger and more formidable than her feeble, would-be seducer. The first edition of the novel had read: "She was more than five feet tall"—certainly not an uncommon height. Later Alarcón increased her stature to more than two *varas* (over five foot six)—tall for a Spanish woman of that time.[12] Alarcón adds three metaphors to emphasize her size: "She was like a giant Niobe, though she had borne no children; a Hercules . . . in skirts [*un Hercules . . . hembra*]; a Roman matron such as you may still see in Trastevere" (p. 447). The two classical allusions have an amusingly incongruous note to them. Alarcón first compares the childless miller's wife to Niobe, the Queen of Thebes, who had fourteen children, and then to Hercules, but again he qualifies it by saying she was a female version of the mythological hero. The third, more obscure allusion, to the typically traditional Trastevere quarter of Rome, is a reminiscence, no doubt, of his trip to Italy.

The characterizations of Lucas and the corregidor are among the most successful parts of the book. In the chapter "A Man Seen from Without and Within," Alarcón employs a clever conceit. After first describing Lucas's homely exterior appearance—short, stoop-shouldered, sparse of beard, with a large nose and ears—Alarcón mentions his attractive features, his well-shaped mouth and perfect teeth. He then passes to Lucas's interior, through his mouth to his vibrant voice, to his discreet and persuasive speech, and finally to the nobility of his character, his courage, loyalty, and honorableness.

The portrait of the corregidor is, if anything, even more vivid. Alarcón elaborates on his colorful dress—the scarlet cape, dove-colored waistcoat, black silk breeches, white stockings, black shoes with gold buckles, sword with a steel guard, stick with tassels, straw-colored gloves which he grasped as if they were a symbol of office, and, of course, the three-cornered hat. Alarcón then passes on to his physical appearance—middle-aged, frail, hunchbacked, toothless, lame, "with a manner of walking *sui generis* (swaying from side to side and back and forth), which can only be described by the absurd formula that he seemed to be lame in both legs at once" (p. 450). The only redeeming feature is the remnants of the good looks he had as a young man. His physical appearance, contrasting with his flamboyant dress, parodies the traditional Don Juan. His mechanical motions suggest those of a marionette. *El sombrero de tres picos* was a natural subject for a ballet, as Manuel de Falla was to prove half a century later.

The corregidora, who had married the dissolute corregidor because of family pressure, does not appear until the end of the novel. After describing her in a traditional way as a dignified woman of austere beauty, Alarcón concludes with a weak metaphor: "more suited to the Christian brush than the pagan chisel" (p. 472). His vignettes of the two male characters are certainly superior to those of their wives.

V   The Corregidor in Action: Comic Effects

Having introduced his three principal characters, Alarcón proceeds in the chapter "The Bombardment of Pamplona" to the opening skirmish between the corregidor and Frasquita, which ends with his total embarrassment. The title suggests in a burlesque way the subject of the chapter, for she is from Pamplona and he is beleaguering her. The repartee between them is cleverly handled. He keeps repeating how much he likes her. She needles him about the corregidora and makes a complete fool of him, catching him up in contradictions. " 'What? Don't you like the corregidora then?' asked Frasquita. . . . 'What a pity! My Lucas told me that he had the pleasure of seeing and talking to her when he went to repair your bedroom clock, and that she is very pretty, very pleasant, and kind.' " Hardly able to deny this statement, the corregidor hedges: "Not so much! Not so much!" She then takes the opposite tack: "On the other hand, others have told me . . . that she is very bad-tempered and jealous, and that you tremble before her as if she were a green switch (que V. le tiembla más que a una vara verde)." The corregidor, blushing, can only repeat: "Not so much, woman. . . . Not so much and not so little." Then, when she asks him point-blank whether he loves his wife, at a loss for an answer the poor man comes forth with a preposterous comparison: "I love her a lot, or, to put it better, I did before I met you. But ever since I laid eyes on you, I don't know what has come over me. . . . All I can tell you is that nowadays if I pat my wife's cheek, for instance, I feel as though I were patting my own. But to touch your hand, your arm, your chin, your waist, I would give all I have in the world!" (p. 453).

The corregidor puts his words into action and tries to seize her arm, whereupon she gives him a push and topples him over backwards, chair and all. Lucas, who had been hiding all this time in the grape arbor above, looks down. And Alarcón comments on the scene: "One might have said that his Honor was the Devil, defeated, not by St. Michael, but by another devil from Hell" (p. 454). Alarcón has transposed the allusion for humorous effect. The corregidor has been changed from a menacing dragon into a devil, who is vanquished by Lucas, another ugly devil rather than St. Michael, who is traditionally portrayed as a handsome knight.[13]

After this initial rebuff, the corregidor sets out in earnest to seduce Frasquita. This amorous campaign of his makes up well over a third of the novel. Garduña, a little like the *gracioso* in the Golden Age comedies, plans the operation for his master. The sprightly dialogue brings out Garduña's obsequiousness and shows the corregidor for what he is, an unprincipled and ineffectual would-be tyrant. The corregidor is aware that he is demeaning himself by having the *alguacil* as his confidant. Each time Garduña makes a comment, the corregidor berates him. Garduña momentarily falls silent and salutes, but then the corregidor continues asking his advice. Garduña is speaking:

"Then let's get down to work, your Honor! I have already told you my plan. All we have to do is to carry it out this very night."
"I have told you time and again that I am not in need of advice," shouted Don Eugenio, suddenly remembering that he was talking with an inferior.
"I thought your Honor asked me for it," stammered Garduña.
"Don't talk back."
Garduña saluted. (p. 457)

A few hours later, after the corregidor has fallen into the water and been admitted into the mill, Frasquita, on her way to Juan López's, crosses paths with Lucas, who is returning to the mill. Each thinks his spouse is an enemy and they avoid each other, but their astute donkeys recognize each other and bray. The title of the chapter, "*Voces clamantes in deserto*" (Voices Crying in the Wilderness), is ironic, since the poetic and prophetic Latin phrase (found in both Isaiah and Matthew) is here applied to animals, and donkeys at that. The scene will turn out to have structural significance in the novel, as later on Frasquita adduces it as proof to Lucas of her innocence. At the time he thought she was in bed with the corregidor, the forthright woman had foiled the latter's insidious scheme and was looking for her husband.

Soon afterwards, when Frasquita returns to the mill with Garduña, Juan López, and Toñuelo, they are met by the corregidor dressed in Lucas's clothes. Toñuelo, confusing the corregidor with Lucas, sets upon him. Frasquita rushes in to protect her supposed husband, and Garduña also joins the fray. By the time the case of mistaken identity is cleared up, Juan López is standing over the prostrate corregidor with his foot on the small of his back. A similar farcical scene occurs in the following chapter when the corregidora's servants dash out of the house and pummel the corregidor and his henchmen.

Throughout the novel Alarcón inserts amusing touches. The millers had preposterously taught a parrot to tell time by reading a sundial. The afternoon the corregidor comes calling earlier than usual, hoping to find her alone, Frasquita, fully aware of his lascivious intentions, needles him about his early arrival. He protests, claiming that it is all of 3:30, whereupon the parrot gives him the lie by calling out a quarter past two.

Alarcón makes use of the fable of the fox and the grapes to ridicule the thwarted corregidor. In the fable, the fox is unable to reach some grapes high up on a vine and rationalizes that they are no doubt green (sour). At the *tertulia* the corregidor passes a bunch of grapes to the bishop, and, casting a quick glance at the miller's wife, adds that he himself hasn't sampled them yet. Another *tertuliano*, an academician comments: "Not, however, because they are green like those in the fable!" The bishop corrects him: "Those in the fable were not green, my learned friend, but out of reach of the fox." The quip hits home, and the corregidor turns livid with anger (p. 455).

Alarcón occasionally uses literary, historical, and mythological allusions in an exaggerated or slightly incongruous manner for comic effect. This was also a favorite device of Valera's. We have already mentioned the references to Niobe, to Hercules, and to St. Michael and the dragon. At the end of the novel the corregidor demands that his wife tell him what transpired between her and the miller, striking his staff on the ground like Antaeus to command attention. Antaeus, who received strength from the earth, was invincible until Hercules held him aloft so that he could not touch the ground and then strangled him. No one, least of all his wife, pays any attention to the corregidor. His blustering is of no avail.

Upon two occasions Alarcón employs a popular expression involving the word *harina* (flour). In the preface, before beginning the story proper, he says: *Conque metámonos ya en harina* (Let's get down to business, p.444). Then, toward the end of the novel when Lucas is reassured about Frasquita's innocence and starts to embrace her, she, still uncertain as to what has gone on between him and the corregidora, objects: *¡Esa es harina de otro costal!* (That is a horse of another color; literally, that is flour from another sack. p.477). Given Lucas's occupation, the expressions are doubly appropriate.

As far as the corregidor is concerned, the novel ends on a completely cynical, though humorous, note. When his wife banishes him from her bedroom for life, he murmurs between his gums (for he has no teeth): "I didn't expect to get off so easily!" The first edition then read: *Garduña me buscará otra* (Garduña will find me another woman). Alarcón later changed it to: *¡Garduña me buscará acomodo!* (Garduña will find me accommodation! p. 479). In this case the earlier version was the more forceful.

The basic situation—a decrepit and lecherous old man thwarted when he tries to seduce a young, attractive, and stalwart woman who is more than a match for him—is an amusing one, and Alarcón made the most of the story's possibilities. A short novel, divided into brief chapters, the action moves rapidly. Alarcón did not give himself the space to develop well-rounded characters, but this was not his forte anyway. With a few deft strokes he made Lucas and the corregidor, and especially Garduña among the secondary characters, come to life. The picturesque setting of the early years of the century allows Alarcón to poke good-natured fun at the backward conditions in Spain. The tone is ironical, never satirical. Then Alarcón enhances the comic effect by a series of devices—occasional farcical scenes, lively repartee, and language which is amusingly to the point. The Romantic bombast found in many of his works is altogether absent. There is scarcely a discordant note to the novel.

VI *Critical Reaction*

El sombrero de tres picos met with instantaneous favor when first published, and its popularity has continued unabated to this day. In his *Historia de mis libros* Alarcón claimed: "Many times I almost felt animosity and repugnance for the work [*la pícara obra*] which had been so universally well received, attributing its good fortune to its insipidity and insignificance." This disparaging remark should not be taken seriously, for Alarcón goes on to say with obvious pride that, by then (1883), it had been translated into Portuguese, German, Russian, French, Italian, English, and Rumanian, and that two comic operettas, one French and the other Belgian, had been based on it (p. 20). Since then, new editions and translations have continued to proliferate. It has, for example, been translated at least nine times into English. It was twice made into a musical comedy, once by Giró in 1893, a second time by González Pastor, Borras, and Lleó in 1917; and three times into operas, once as *Der Corregidor* in German in 1896, with music by Hugo Wolf and text by Rosa Mayreder, in Italian in 1933 as *La farsa amorosa*, with music by Riccardo Zandonai and libretto by Arturo Rossato, and again in German, as *Die Zwillingsesel* (The Twin Donkeys) by Erwin Dressel in 1932. In 1919 de Falla's ballet with libretto by Martínez Sierra, sets by Picasso, and choreography by Massine was a huge success in London. There have been at least three dramatic adaptations of the theme, *La feria de Cuernicabra* by Alfredo Mañas, *La pícara molinera* by Juan Ignacio Luca de Tena, and Casona's *La Molinera de Arcos* (1947).[14]

El sombrero de tres picos is the one work of Alarcón's which has met with universal praise from the critics as well as from the public. Luis Alfonso reviewed it favorably when it first appeared. He pointed out that its popular tone contrasted with Alarcón's earlier, more artificial stories. It was he who coined the often-quoted phrase that Alarcón *ha solido en ciertos momentos mojar la pluma de Quevedo en la paleta de Goya* (He moistened Quevedo's pen in Goya's palette).[15] Alfonso's colorful metaphor is perhaps more striking than it is accurate, because, although *El sombrero de tres picos* has much in common with Goya's cartoons, Alarcón never falls into Quevedo's bitter satirical vein. The often caustic Revilla, who was not given to panegyrics, acclaimed the novel as a "true jewel."[16] In an article first published in the *Revista Europea*, Palacio Valdés praised its lively humor and said that it was an authentic product of the region where it was written.[17] Pardo Bazán called *El sombrero de tres picos* "the king of Spanish tales" (*el rey de los cuentos españoles*).[18] Of Alarcón's contemporaries, Valera was perhaps the least enthusiastic about the novel. According to him, Lucas's projected revenge lacked verisimilitude, for the upright miller was acting out of character when he set out to seduce the corregidora. Valera went so far as to claim *El Niño de la Bola* to be a superior novel.[19] In recent years all the critics who have written about Alarcón, including Montesinos, Gullón, and Vicente Gaos, are in general agreement that *El sombrero de tres picos* is the one novel of Alarcón's which does not date; in Montesinos's words it is "his only undisputed success."[20]

CHAPTER 9

El escándalo

I *Theme and Characters*

DURING the 1870s, with the greater freedom that came with the overthrow of Isabel II and the subsequent Restoration, religion began to receive a lot of outspoken scrutiny in the Spanish novel.[1] In 1874, the skeptical Valera poked good-natured fun at his ingenuous clerics, Luis and the vicar, in *Pepita Jiménez*. Although the author emphasized that Luis's vocation was false and that he would have made a bad priest, some readers saw in the novel an intimation that marriage was a more natural way of life than the priesthood. The anticlerical bias was unmistakable in Galdós's so-called unholy trinity, *Doña Perfecta* (1876), *Gloria* (1877), and *La familia de León Roch* (1879). *El escándalo* (1875) was the most vociferous answer of the conservatives and neo-Catholics to this challenge.

In his *Historia de mis libros* Alarcón writes about the genesis of the novel. The subject had been in his mind as early as 1863, and he had begun writing it in 1868, but after finishing two chapters, he was interrupted by the outbreak of the Revolution. He did not get back to the novel until six years later. Once again he was disrupted, this time by the Restoration, with the novel less than half finished. In May 1875 his children came down with the whooping cough, and Alarcón took the whole family to the Escorial, hoping in vain that the mountain air would be beneficial. The youngest child died shortly after their arrival, and the family stayed on to be near his grave. Alarcón claims that he would go to bed at sunset, sleep until one, get up and write until eight in the morning. He would then spend the day with his friends, who could not understand how he had written a novel in four weeks when they never saw him working. Once again Alarcón wants us to believe that he worked at a superhuman rate when moved by inspiration. Martínez Kleiser quotes from a letter Alarcón wrote on August 18, 1874: *"El escándalo*, a major work, will be out within a month" (p. xxiii), which suggests the novel was well on the way before his sojourn at the Escorial and that he only put the finishing touches on it there.

El escándalo is the story of the exemplary conversion and reform of a young rake. Alarcón quotes the definition of the word *escándalo* from the academy dictionary as an epigraph at the beginning, and then he keeps repeating the word during the course of the novel. The protagonist, Fabián Conde, indeed behaves scandalously, seducing any woman who strikes his fancy and then boasting about his conquests. His reputation is such that his reformation is not taken seriously. His previous licentious life returns to haunt him.

Like *El final de Norma, El escándalo* is divided into books, eight in all. The novel opens with Fabián Conde frantically driving a carriage through the jeering carnival throngs in Madrid on Shrove Monday. He bursts into a convent and in a frenzy he begs a Jesuit priest for counsel. Fabián's confession, the story of his life until then, takes up the next five sections.

When he was fourteen, his mother, on her deathbed, informed him that his father, a general, had died in disgrace, stripped of his title and inheritance, for having betrayed to the Carlists the fortified town he was defending. After finishing his education, the protagonist, under the assumed name of Fabián Conde, had devoted himself to a life of debauchery. One day, an unsavory individual, Gutiérrez, who had been his father's lieutenant during the war, appeared, told him what had really occurred, and offered to rehabilitate his name for a price. The general, in fact, had been carrying on a clandestine affair with Beatriz, the wife of the governor of the city. The latter arranged to have the Carlists intercept the general on his way to a rendezvous. He was killed bravely resisting the enemy, and Beatriz subsequently committed suicide. Everyone accepted the governor's lie that the general had been bought by the Carlists.

During this period Fabián had two close friends. Diego, a foundling with no family, who was envious of Fabián's social position and of his success with women, nevertheless became his confidant. Lázaro, whose background was even more enigmatic, did not take part in their frivolous life, but devoted himself to helping others.

When Fabián consulted Lázaro about Gutiérrez's proposition, the latter urged him to reject it. He pointed out that although Fabián's father was not a traitor, the whole story could not be exposed without tarnishing Beatriz's reputation. Fabián sensed that Lázaro was right but selfishly spurned his advice and even broke off his friendship with him. Gutiérrez blackmailed the former governor, who had become a prominent politician, and Fabián recovered his title and inheritance.

Fabián, then twenty-six, embarked on a tempestuous affair with Matilde, the thirty-five-year-old wife of a general currently exiled to the Canary Islands, but he soon fell in love with her young and innocent niece, Gabriela, who lived with her. Matilde was jealous, but when her husband suddenly returned to Madrid, she decided to bow out of the picture in order to allay his suspicions. She told Fabián to marry Gabriela. Fabián, grateful to Matilde but also remembering his former passion, embraced her. Gabriela witnessed the scene from the next room and fainted. Fabián's hopes were dashed. Gabriela entered a convent, and he resumed his scandalous ways. After a time, he had a change of heart and, resolving to merit Gabriela, accepted a post in the Spanish legation in London where he behaved in an exemplary manner. Diego, acting as Fabián's guarantor, made arrangements with Gabriela's father for their marriage, neglecting to mention, of course, that Fabián had had an affair with his brother's wife. Fabián returned from London, and the marriage was about to take place.

In the meanwhile, Diego had married. Upon first meeting Gregoria, Fabián had trouble hiding his distaste for this vulgar, *cursi* woman. On a subsequent visit he found her alone. She accused him of wanting to seduce her, and he left after an acrimonious exchange. Diego refused to accept Fabián's explanation. Challenging Fabián to a duel, he said he would tell Gabriela's father about Matilde and would expose Fabián's chicanery in obtaining his father's patrimony.

It is at this point that the distraught Fabián rushes to consult Father Manrique. According to the Jesuit, Fabián must refuse to fight Diego. He must give up all claim to Gabriela; he does not deserve her after committing adultery with her aunt. He must renounce his title and inheritance; he cannot legitimately claim them without exposing his father's adulterous affair with Beatriz and sullying the honor of both families. Fabián, the former profligate atheist, suddenly becomes converted and agrees to the priest's self-sacrificing penance.

In the last two sections the narration shifts to the third person. The omniscient Alarcón, not Fabián, is now the narrator. Fabián goes to the home of Lázaro, whom he has not seen for many months. There he encounters Lázaro's stepbrother, Juan, who recounts to him Lázaro's past life. Years before, when Lázaro was visiting his parents in Chile, his stepmother accused him of making advances. He made no effort to defend himself and was disowned by his father. On her deathbed, the stepmother had confessed to Juan that it was she who had been in love with Lázaro and who had been spurned by him. To gain revenge she had maligned him. Lázaro had borne the calumny with stoic forbearance. If he had divulged the truth, his father, who was deeply in love with his wife, would have been crushed. Fabián now realizes how badly he had misjudged his friend.

Fabián's heroic renunciation convinces Diego of his friend's innocence and of Gregoria's guilt. Diego first threatens to kill her but forgives her when she melodramatically confides that she is pregnant. Shortly thereafter, Fabián is summoned by Diego, who has suffered a severe attack of hemoptysis. Before dying, he makes Fabián promise to marry Gabriela. In the epilogue, which takes place a month later, Fabián, who twice had been on the point of winning Gabriela, finally sees his hopes realized. At the last moment Alarcón altered the course of the novel and tacked on a happy ending. Gabriela's father even rationalizes away Fabián's adulterous conduct with Matilde by saying that she had been the aggressor. This piece of casuistry contrasts markedly with the rigid ethical standards promulgated elsewhere in the novel.

Alarcón makes his didactic message abundantly clear. Several times Father Manrique interrupts Fabián's confession to moralize, and Gabriela, Lázaro, and even Fabián himself at the end express equally austere ideas. The advice given to Fabián first by Lázaro and later by Manrique is draconian. Lázaro's forbearance, when he refuses to defend himself against his stepmother's calumny, seems excessive; and the same can be said about Fabián's magnanimity in giving away most of his fortune at the end of the book. One can understand how the readers were polarized by the novel. The ultramontane conservatives found it inspirational; the liberals, overdrawn and unduly pious.

Baquero Goyanes compared the eleventh edition of *El escándalo* (1891), the last one published during Alarcón's lifetime, with the first (1875), and indicated the principal variants. In general, the changes are not of major importance. The most significant ones are those in which Alarcón strengthened the didactic and Catholic tone of some of Manrique's and Gabriela's speeches.[2]

Harriet Powers has pointed out how Alarcón uses religious allegory to reinforce his characterizations.[3] According to Fabián, the opening scene with the crowd in the Puerta del Sol mocking him occurred at the hour of the Final Judgment. His interview with Manrique, which will alter the course of his life, is about to begin. Gabriela's surname is significantly "de la Guardia," and Fabián frequently refers to her as his guardian angel. Several biblical images bring out the evil in Gregoria. She is alternately referred to as Eve, the serpent, and the devil.[4] Alarcón leaves few stones unturned to make his message come through.

El escándalo has four subplots which are intertwined to give scope to the principal intrigue, Fabián's conversion and reformation: 1) the death and dishonor of Fabián's father; 2) Fabián's adulterous affair with Matilde and his falling in love with Gabriela; 3) the story of Lázaro; 4) Fabián's friendship with Diego and Gregoria's jealous attempt to destroy him.

Fabián's father had been falsely accused of betraying the Isabelline party, but he was guilty of having an adulterous affair with the wife of a subordinate. Similarly, Fabián, although innocent of having designs on Gregoria, had led a licentious life and had committed adultery with Matilde. He had, also, with Gutiérrez's help, regained his title and inheritance through trickery. The story of Lázaro offers a parallel to the counsel given to Fabián by Manrique. Lázaro refused to defend himself from his stepmother's libelous accusations and then devoted himself in a Christlike manner to helping the poor. This is what Fabián, at Manrique's urging, was preparing to do until Diego, in a *deus ex machina* gesture on his deathbed, brought Fabián and Gabriela together again. Lázaro's stepmother behaved much like Gregoria, although from different motives, the former from unrequited passion, the latter from jealous insecurity.

Diego and Gregoria are among the most interesting characters in the novel, and Manrique, in a conversation with Fabián, analyzes them perceptively. Diego, a foundling, was always jealous of Fabián's position and his success with the opposite sex. It was essential to him that Fabián find Gregoria attractive, and he immediately sensed that Fabián saw her for what she was. Aware of her own inferiority, she wanted to attract her husband's friend and then repulse him so as to prove that she was as desirable as, but more virtuous than, the aristocratic women who had fallen prey to him. When Fabián scorned her, she sought revenge, and her husband, also jealous of Fabián's past successes, all too readily believed her.

Alarcón's statement in his *Historia de mis libros* that "*El escándalo* is rigorously historical" (p. 23) has led critics to seek models for the characters. Monroe Hafter sees a similarity between Alarcón and his protagonist.[5] Alarcón's family lived in straitened circumstances, and he had to make his own way. Similarly, Fabián had lost his title and his inheritance. Alarcón led a bohemian life as a member of the *Cuerda granadina* and the *Colonia granadina*, and then embarked on his short-lived, tempestuous career as editor of *El Látigo*, which ended in the duel. Pardo Bazán saw a similarity between Alarcón's transformation from a youthful radical to a staid conservative and Fabián's conversion and reformation.[6] According to Alarcón (p. 22), Father Manrique was based on a Jesuit he had known, but he does not identify him. Martínez Kleiser states that the deathbed reconciliation scene between Fabián and Diego had actually occurred, although he does not identify the latter figure, who is supposed to have said to Alarcón: "Write down those things. I want everybody to know them, as a lesson for them and as a punishment for me" (p. xxiii). In a series of articles Gamallo Fierros postulated that Nicomedes Pastor Díaz was the original for Diego. Alarcón had been present at Pastor Díaz's death in 1863, and they had presumably become reconciled at that time. Martínez Kleiser took exception to Gamallo Fierros's hypothesis, and a polemic ensued.[7] Montensinos, in his essay "Sobre *El escándolo* de Alarcón," reviewed the evidence and expressed doubts as to whether Alarcón had ever broken with Pastor Díaz in the first place. Moreover, Diego had little in common with the author of *De Villahermosa a la China*.[8] We will never know with certainty to what extent Alarcón based his characters on actual models, but it would actually contribute little to our understanding or appreciation of the novel if we did.

II   *Romantic Elements*

Alarcón's first novel, *El final de Norma,* was a melodramatic story of adventure laid in an exotic setting. In *El sombrero de tres picos* he retold a comic, popular tale. *El escándalo,* like *El Niño de la Bola* and *La Pródiga,* which were to follow, is an entirely different type of novel. Alarcón has become a moralist with a message to expound. The tone is serious, almost humorless. In these novels he studies certain problems of contemporary Spanish society and, in the process, analyzes his characters psychologically. Yet, his Romantic affinities are still very much present.   .

Fabián Conde, to whom all women are fair prey, is a typical Romantic hero in the tradition of Byron and Don Juan Tenorio. In the first chapter he is characterized: "In the Athens of Lord Byron he might very well have served as Don Juan. In fact, he resembled all the Romantic heroes of the great poet of the age, which is as much as to say that he also resembled the poet himself" (p. 482). When Gabriela takes refuge in a convent, Fabián has recourse to a frantic round of debauchery, which eclipses, he almost boastingly says, "the daring and impiety of Don Juan Tenorio and Lord Byron" (p. 537). Alarcón appears to have ambivalent feelings about his protagonist's amorous exploits. On the one hand, he seems almost envious, while the moralist in him can only condemn them. It is Zorrilla's hero, not Tirso's, that Alarcón cites here. Nowhere in the novel is the latter mentioned. Alarcón was not concerned with the theological problem of salvation. As in the case of Don Juan Tenorio, it is which brings about Fabián's conversion, but, unlike Zorrilla's protagonist, he reforms in time to gain happiness in this world, not merely redemption in the next.

Like so many Romantic protagonists, Alarcón's three principal, male characters have mysterious backgrounds. Diego is a foundling, and his origin is never clarified. Fabián finds out the true story about his father only partway through the novel. Lázaro keeps his past life a secret until his brother divulges it at the end. The reader's interest is whetted by these obscurities and enigmas.

There are frequent abrupt changes and sudden illuminations during the course of the novel. A character is presented in one light, and then we discover that we did not know the truth, or the whole truth. Again Fabián's father and Lázaro are cases in point. The plot engages attention by swiftly interposing successes and setbacks. When Matilde tells Fabián that Gabriela is in love with him, he is overjoyed, but Matilde is not ready to bow selflessly out of the picture until her husband appears and becomes suspicious of her relations with Fabián. Now she is afraid and wants at all cost to quell his jealousy. Fabián foolishly scotches his chances with Gabriela by embracing Matilde. Later, with Matilde out of the picture, Diego patches up Fabián's relations with Gabriela. Although Fabián's past conduct had been less than exemplary, he has reformed, and he is genuinely in love. A happy ending seems possible. But Gregoria's insecure vanity causes her to turn her husband against his erstwhile friend. Again Fabián seems to have lost Gabriela, this time for good. Diego's change of heart on his deathbed alters the situation a final time. Although Alarcón has analyzed Diego perceptively, his repeated shifts of loyalty seem contrived. From Fabián's best friend, he turns into his worst enemy, intent on destroying him. Then, at the end, he brings Fabián and Gabriela back together again. Similarly, Fabián's metamorphosis is somewhat implausible. Granted, when he came to Manrique, he was fraught with emotion. He was fully aware how despicable his past conduct had been, and he did not want to fight a duel with his former friend. But his transformation seems abrupt. He immediately agrees to renounce Gabriela and his title, to give his fortune to the poor, even to go to prison for having connived to regain his patrimony. Although these melodramatic reversals do not bear up well under analysis, they no doubt contributed to the success of the novel. The reader is caught up in the events and does not question the lack of verisimilitude in the characterizations.

Fabián does not behave consistently. At one point he and Diego go to a bar and he tries unsuccessfully to pacify his friend. Finally, exasperated, Fabián blurts out the truth: "I don't like Gregoria! I think you made a mistake marrying her! She is an abominable woman who is going to cost you your life!" (p. 566). How could he expect to become reconciled with Diego after this tactless outburst? After his interview with Manrique, Fabián writes telling Diego the heroic sacrifices he is making. Again he mentions his antipathy for Gregoria and cruelly tells his friend he is going to die. When Lázaro returns and reports that Diego has pardoned him, Fabián again reacts bitterly. Christian charity is forgotten. "So this fool recognizes his infamy and my innocence! So the executioner begs my pardon! It's too late! . . . I'll never forgive him! . . . Now I'm the one who demands blood!" (p. 602). Manrique reproves him, and Fabián subsides. His dislike of Gregoria and his disillusion when Diego turns against him are understandable, but his abrupt changes are not well motivated. Throughout his life Fabián has behaved selfishly, intent on getting what he wants. Even in the moments when he is trying to act magnanimously, the darker side of his nature keeps coming to the surface. These scenes do portray a better-rounded character, one who is not all of a piece, but they lead us to wonder whether his conversion had been that complete.

Another aspect of Romanticism, a sentimental lachrymosity, keeps slipping into the novel. The early Fabián is a calculating philanderer unconcerned about the havoc his amorous adventures may cause. But then, after falling in love with Gabriela, he changes. He frequently dissolves into tears. He is described upon first meeting Manrique: "There was something infantile and imbecile in the way he acted, the result of many emotions which had been pent up until then and which were about to burst forth in tears and moaning" (p. 486). Before leaving for London, Fabián embraces Diego, and they burst out crying like two children. When Fabián first meets Gabriela's father, overcome with emotion at his impending marriage, he again weeps.

Alarcón frequently groups his characters in theatrical poses in moments of emotional stress. Matilde, weeping bitterly, tells Fabián and Gabriela that they are free to get married. Fabián describes the scene in a falsely sentimental manner, for what did Matilde actually feel? ":Then Gabriela, also weeping, threw herself into Matilde's arms and covered her face with kisses, while I entered the parlor and cast myself at the feet of that tender group, who represented all the affection of my heart" (p. 531). Another scene where Alarcón overplays the emotions occurs at the end of the novel. After Fabián reads the letter in which Diego asks for his forgiveness, Alarcón describes his reaction: "He listened with a beaming countenance and with his eyes raised toward heaven, while he stretched one hand to Lázaro and the other to the Jesuit, who, in turn, affectionately drew Juan to him so that he might join in the happiness and glory of this triumphant group" (p. 608). We are reminded of *El hijo pródigo*, written almost twenty years earlier. Alarcón in these scenes falls into bathos akin to the eighteenth-century *comédie larmoyante* or the paintings of Greuze.

Alarcón at times handles dramatic scenes in an overblown, Romantic manner. Fabián describes himself in his youthful, libertine days in Madrid: "I remember that I was successively the illegitimate brother of a petty German king, the sacrilegious son of a Roman cardinal, the leader of a European gang of swindlers, a secret agent of the Emperor of France, a second Monte Cristo, the owner of diamond mines, and so on. And amid all this they continued calling me Fabián Conde, which was how my calling cards read" (p. 491). At the time, Fabián was a young rake, living comfortably off his mother's inheritance. His various incognitos are all exaggerated. Did anyone really think he was any of those Romantic personages?

When Fabián consults Lázaro after Gutiérrez's visit, his friend urges him to reject the shady proposition and concludes: "Inherit, Fabián, the grievances and sadness of your innocent mother, not the title and wealth of the ingrate who embittered her existence! Don't be happier than that unfortunate woman! Don't leave her alone, offended and unavenged, with no friend to mourn for her, in that obscure grave which no one but you has bathed with tears!" (p. 515). Again the advice is austere, and the language is wildly extravagant. Should Fabián renounce a title and wealth he is entitled to simply because his mother had been unhappy? Would she have wanted him to?

After Fabián loses Gabriela the first time because of his indiscreet behavior with Matilde, he reverts to a life of debauchery. He later explains his conduct to Manrique:

Pero faltábanme fuerzas (o, a lo menos, tal me lo imaginaba) para marchar a solas por el áspero sendero de la virtud, y de aquí el que, con objeto de no oir los gritos de mis remordimientos, acábase siempre en mis recaídas por buscar el estruendo del mundo, el vocerío del escándalo, el vértigo de la orgía, el delirio de la embriaguez, hasta conseguir aturdirme, ensordecer, embrutecerme, o, cuando menos, no tener tiempo ni ocio para pensar en mi pobre alma. (p. 537)

(But I lacked the courage—or at least so I imagined—to walk alone the rough path of virtue, and in my determination to close my ears to the cries of my remorse, whenever I fell anew, I'd always seek the turmoil of the world, the vociferation of scandal, the dizziness of orgy, the delirium of drunkeness, until I'd become bewildered, deaf, brutalized, or at least have no time or leisure to think of my poor soul.)

The sentence, with its grandiloquent tone, is in the nineteenth-century rhetorical tradition. It ends with two series of parallel expressions. In the first, *el estruendo del mundo*, etc., Alarcón strings together four substantives, each followed by a prepositional phrase. Then follow the four infinitives depending on *conseguir: aturdirme, ensordecer, embrutecerme,* and finally *tener. Tener,* in turn, has two noun objects: *tiempo* and *ocio.* The self-pity in the final phrase, *mi pobre alma,* rings hollow. Why should the reader feel sorry for Fabián? After all, he did bring his troubles on himself.

Alarcón tends to fall into the trite and conventional, particularly when describing Gabriela. Early in the novel, as she first begins to blossom into womanhood, she is portrayed as an embodiment of the Christian ideal: "This mysterious, unconscious, and instinctively modest beauty inspired an invincible respect and did not appear bold and provocative like the Greek goddess, but soft and venerable like Christian virgins, as chaste as they are beautiful, who prefer heaven to earth and whose images are honored on altars" (p. 522). Gabriela is so etherealized, especially in the second simile, "soft and venerable like Christian virgins," and is so lacking in plastic appeal that she scarcely seems to be a creature of flesh and blood.

In the epilogue Alarcón again describes Gabriela, this time at her wedding: "Never had an angel of heaven been invested with so graceful and superb a human form, and never had the classic beauty dreamed of by paganism reflected so intensely the splendors of the immortal spirit for which this incomparable figure served as receptacle" (p. 611). The phrases "angel of heaven" and "immortal spirit" suggest Gabriela's Christian virtues. The adjectives "graceful" and "superb" give a sensual touch to the description, while the phrase "classic beauty dreamed of by paganism" likens her to a classical statue. Alarcón intimates that Gabriela will be all things to Fabián, but to express this idea he has had recourse to a series of clichés, ending with the banal metaphor "for which this incomparable figure served as receptacle."

At times Alarcón writes with bombast. And frequently he has recourse to hackneyed stereotypes. His Romantic affinities continue to manifest themselves even in a novel in which he sought to break new ground.

El escándalo is a serious novel, almost without humor and with only occasional touches of irony. Early in the novel, when Fabián is involved in his adulterous affair with Matilde, Gabriela is attracted to him but does not yet realize how deep her feelings are. Almost too ingenuously she asks: "Aunt, people are going to imagine Fabián is in love with you when they notice that he never leaves the house. But then, when I'm older, everybody will say he's my sweetheart. How we'll laugh!" Or again: "Aunt, why is it that you're always opposed to having me tell my parents in my letters how very kind Fabián is to us?" (p. 521). Both Matilde and Fabián are, of course, well aware of the irony in her naive questions.

Upon returning from England, Fabián rushes to Diego's house where he meets Gregoria for the first time. He immediately sees her for what she is, a presumptuous bourgeoise. Inhospitably, she had not prepared dinner for him, much to her husband's embarrassment. She proceeds to needle Fabián about his past life as a rake and says she hopes he will not behave that way with Gabriela. Both she and, more surprisingly, Diego miss the cutting irony, which is closer to sarcasm, in Fabián's reply: "Even if I still were evil, the picture of domestic bliss I have before my eyes, the sweet confidence that reigns here, the respect that even the words of this affectionate servant inspire, the delights, never experienced by me, which I have just divined between you two, and above all, Diego, the strict virtue and lofty character of your noble wife would serve me as edification, example, and stimulus to be a model husband and bring to Gabriela as much happiness as my new sister Gregoria gives you" (p. 550). The next day Gregoria does invite Fabián for dinner. She harshly upbraids the servant for her ineptitude, fends off Fabián's imagined slights, and defensively claims she is inferior to no one:

I omit Gregoria's sharp reprimands to the maid each time she transgressed, in Gregoria's judgment, against the rules of polite society in the manner of serving the food, in presenting the dishes, or in calling attention to the things they had sent in from the inn and which Francisca had never seen before. Nor shall I mention the thousand pointless interpellations and excuses my friend's wife made to me to show me she knew how to forestall the criticisms and censures which, in reality, hadn't occurred to me at all, or to make me believe that she didn't envy anything she didn't have in her house, that she had nothing to learn from the most elegant aristocrats, and that she didn't consider herself inferior to me in good taste, or to Gabriela in virtue, or to Charlemagne in majesty, or to Socrates in wisdom. (p. 551)

Baquero Goyanes compares this scene to the famous banquet in Larra's sketch "El castellano viejo," but there is a world of difference between the two.[9] Alarcón sarcastically exposes Gregoria's false pretentiousness, which is a mask for her insecurity. The passage ends with the preposterous comparisons to Charlemagne and Socrates. Absent is the accumulation of hyperbolic detail found in Larra (or in many descriptions of Galdós). Alarcón's scene is not truly comical. He did not take full advantage of the opportunity to ridicule a *cursi* and basically despicable character like Gregoria.

III   *Critical Reaction*

When *El escándalo* came out on July 1, 1875, it attracted immediate attention, and many of the major critics wrote about it. Late that month Canalejas reviewed it in the *Revista Europea*.[10] He ranked Alarcón among the top contemporary Spanish novelists, but, given his Krausist orientation, he was unsympathetic to Alarcón's religious thesis. He particularly objected to the two principal characters, Fabián and Manrique. Fabián was a weakling, a brother of Valera's Faustino *(Las ilusiones del doctor Faustino)*. Self-indulgent and intent only on pleasure, he was not a representative nineteenth-century liberal and hence not a worthy adversary of Manrique, Alarcón's papal spokesman. Alarcón had stacked the cards in favor of the thesis he had set out to prove. Canalejas also objected to Alarcón's going so far as to select a Jesuit as Fabián's counselor. Any person with religious or ethical standards could have brought out the immorality of Fabián's past life.

Revilla published a mixed review of *El escándalo* in *La Ilustración Española y Americana*. Although critical of Alarcón as a philosopher and thinker, he gave him high marks as an artist. He praised Alarcón's characterizations of Diego, Gregoria, and Gabriela, but was critical of Manrique and found Fabián's sudden conversion after his marathon confession lacking in authenticity. His overall evaluation was decidedly unenthusiastic: "The lack of verisimilitude in some of the situations, the falseness of the characters, . . . the absurd conversation of the protagonist, the awkward narrative form, the exaggerated ultramontane doctrines which Alarcón now espouses, these are the defects of *El escándalo*."[11] Three years later Revilla published an essay on Alarcón in the *Revista Contemporánea* in which he praised *El sombrero de tres picos* and the travel books but treated *El escándalo* even more harshly than before. In particular, the liberal Revilla castigated Alarcón's reactionary ideology: "Neo-Catholicism had a new leader in the literary field, and this leader—it is sad to say!—was a veteran of liberty."[12]

Clarín first mentioned *El escándalo* in a review of Galdós's *Doña Perfecta*. After damning the novel rotundly: "In *El escándalo* Alarcón certainly does not make his mark as a psychologist, or as a profound thinker; he comes forth rather as a daring and eloquent sectarian, but with narrow views and satanical tenacity," Clarín somewhat paradoxically granted that Alarcón had talent as a novelist and had made a significant contribution to the recent revival of the genre in Spain.[13] The following year, he again mentioned *El escándalo*, this time in a review of *Gloria*.[14] He basically followed in the steps of Canalejas's criticism of two years before. The conservatives had an ally in Alarcón, supposedly a philosophical, transcendental novelist, but Clarín accused the author of weighting the scales. Fabián, his protagonist, was no freethinker, but simply an irresponsible young man who, when the time came, was all too ready to reform.

In an article on Alarcón published in the *Revista Europea* in 1878, Palacio Valdés pretty much limited himself to discussing *El sombrero de tres picos* and *El escándalo*, heaping praise on the former and opprobrium on the latter. He admitted that *El escándalo* read well but objected to Alarcón's thesis, facetiously claiming: "There are two things which never in my life have I been able to digest, prawns and Alarcón's philosophy." He went on to accuse the characters, especially the masculine ones, of being false, "crudely carved figures."[15]

Four major critics with liberal leanings had, by and large, assessed *El escándalo* negatively. Although recognizing Alarcón's talents as a storyteller, they objected to his message and to the way he developed it. The hypersensitive Alarcón's feelings were hurt. Some years later in his *Historia de mis libros* (pp. 20–23), he railed back at his critics for castigating what he self-pityingly referred to as his "poor *Escándalo*." He began by stating that it was his most controversial work, the one which had attracted the most praise and the most criticism. It was also his personal favorite. In particular, he took to task the critics (Canalejas and Clarín) who objected to his having chosen as his spokesman a priest, and a Jesuit at that. Palacio Valdés's hostile evaluation of the novel, exacerbated by his flippant tone, also must have hit a raw nerve in Alarcón. But his ill-humored rejoinder hardly made friends for his cause.

In 1891 Pardo Bazán gave a mixed assessment of *El escándalo*.[16] She praised Alarcón's skill as a narrator and found Diego and Gregoria to be the most original characters; Gabriela, Lázaro, Manrique, even Fabián, were more conventional. She was apparently the first to point out the similarities between Fabián and Don Juan Tenorio. Although she did not accuse Alarcón of being a papist, she did find the advice that first Lázaro and then Manrique gave Fabián stoical, more Jansenist that Jesuitical in tone. She said that she had consulted theologians who agreed with her that Fabián had behaved in an orthodox fashion when he had rehabilitated his father's honor and recovered his title and patrimony, even though he had not exposed the adulterous affair with Beatriz. After all, adultery was not a major crime. He had been a brave and loyal officer; that was the essential. It can be said that Alarcón had created a dilemma for Fabián. If Manrique's solution was severe, Pardo Bazán's was casuistical.

That same year the Augustinian Blanco García in his *La literatura española en el siglo XIX* came to the defense of *El escándalo*.[17] He deplored the fact that the ideological conflict between the rationalists and the Catholics which had been polarizing Spain when *El escándalo* appeared had provoked such unjustly fierce attacks on the novel. He himself found it a welcome relief from the excesses of the Naturalists.

During the following decades *El escándalo* continued to be read and new editions kept appearing. But, along with the rest of Alarcón's work, except for *El sombrero de tres picos*, it was largely ignored by the critics, and the occasional comments which are to be found are adverse. Andrés González Blanco concluded his evaluation: "When some critics have considered Don Pedro Antonio de Alarcón as the master of the modern novel, I always think with sadness of *El escándalo*."[18] César Barja's brief analysis of *El escándalo* in *Libros y autores modernos* was equally hostile. He claimed that Alarcón was incapable of constructing a character who behaved coherently, and humorously accused Alarcón of making Fabián "jump like an acrobat."[19]

The most detailed recent study of the novel is Montesinos's long article "Sobre *El escándalo* de Alarcón," a continuation of his 1955 book.[20] Montesinos summarizes the critical reaction to the novel when it first appeared, discusses the similarities between *El escándalo* and Pastor Díaz's *De Villahermosa a la China*, and then analyzes the novel in some detail. His evaluation is perhaps the most negative of them all. The characterizations of Diego and Gregoria were almost the only parts of the novel that found favor in his eyes.

El sombrero de tres picos had been an instantaneous success both with the public and the critics. Alarcón no doubt expected that his third novel, more ambitious in scope and more serious in purpose, would be equally well received. Yet, the early reviews by Canalejas and Revilla were, at best, lukewarm, while Clarín and Palacio Valdés were decidedly hostile. Liberals, they were scarcely going to wax enthusiastic about a novel espousing the reactionary cause. Subsequent critics have largely concurred with their adverse judgment. *El escándalo* is a melodramatic novel arranged to prove the author's thesis. Yet, the novel was warmly received by the public. The first edition sold out within five days, and the novel's popularity has continued almost unabated to this day. The forty-fourth edition in the "Colección de Escritores Castellanos" came out in 1970, and it has recently been edited for the "Clásicos Castellanos" series. Today's readers are probably less concerned with the novel's conservative ideology than they are caught up in its fast-moving plot.

CHAPTER 10

El Niño de la Bola

AFTER *El escándalo*, almost five years elapsed before the publication of the next novel, *El Niño de la Bola.* This was not a productive period of Alarcón's life; only his academy discourse and a few short pieces came out during that interval. Martínez Kleiser, quoting from Alarcón's correspondence, tells us that Alarcón mentioned it as a project he had had in mind as early as February 1875, four months before the completion of *El escándalo.* Two years later he complained of lack of inspiration, of an inability to write; the novel had not even been begun. Somewhat later, however, he was working ten or twelve hours a day on it and was delighted with the way it was going. He finished it in December 1879, and it was published the following month (p. xxiv).

I *Structure*

El Niño de la Bola is the second-longest of Alarcón's novels, about a third shorter than *El escándalo.* Again the novel is divided into books: a short introductory section, three longer ones, and an epilogue which quickly carries the action to the tragic finale. The story begins *in medias res,* in April 1840. After describing the wild and impressive countryside between Guadix and Granada, the author introduces the handsome, mysterious, and extravagantly dressed protagonist, Manuel Venegas. He encounters a heterogeneous group of people traveling together for mutual protection in the opposite direction—several olive-oil merchants, a sacristan, an army officer, two widows, some students returning to the University of Granada. One of the women recognizes Manuel and is about to recount his past life, when the author breaks in and says he himself will do so and spare the reader her muddled account. This opening scene whets the reader's interest in the mysterious protagonist and it also introduces a *costumbrista* note about the perils of traveling in those years. Surprisingly enough, such regionalistic touches are rare in Alarcón's two novels with a contemporary Andalusian setting, *El Niño de la Bola* and *La Pródiga*.

In Book Two, "Antecedents," Alarcón drops back in time to take up the first twenty years of Manuel's life. His father, Rodrigo Venegas, had spent his fortune patriotically fighting the Napoleonic invaders and was heavily in debt to the repulsive usurer Elias López, alias Caifás (the high priest of the Jews who condemned Christ). Although Rodrigo heroically lost his life rushing into Caifás's burning house to save his financial records, the unrelenting moneylender claimed all the family's possessions, leaving the ten-year-old orphan penniless. He was taken in by the simple and kindly parish priest, Trinidad Muley. Signs of instability began to appear in Manuel. For three years he refused to talk to anyone. Then he fell in love with Caifás's beautiful daughter, Soledad, a year and a half his junior, and spent hours outside her house every day hoping to catch a glimpse of her. He managed to speak to her only once, one day on her way home from school. Caifás, who did not want her to have anything to do with Manuel, took her out of school and kept her virtually incarcerated. Manuel acquired a modest fortune by mining for gold and precious stones in the mountains. At the annual *fiesta* held in honor of the "Niño de la Bola," a man can bid to dance with a given girl—another bit of local folklore. Manuel offered his whole fortune to dance with Soledad, but Caifás thwarted him by outbidding him and then threw in his face that Manuel still owed him a million pesos. Manuel swore that he would go off and earn a fortune, return, pay the debt, and marry Soledad, and woe to anyone who set eyes on her in the meanwhile.

In the next section, "The Return of the Absent One," the action shifts forward again to 1840. Just before entering Guadix, Manuel encounters Soledad's mother. In a violently emotional scene she urges him to leave immediately. Manuel finally realizes why—Soledad has married. The crazed Manuel rushes off and spends the night roaming about the countryside. Then a secondary character, Mirabel, a member of one of the leading families in town, recounts to his *tertulia* the circumstances of her marriage. Her father was insistent that she marry before Manuel's return, but only the unattractive Vitriolo dared present himself. When Caifás threatened to make her enter a convent and Antonio Arreguí, a newcomer to the town who was not intimidated by Manuel, asked for her hand, she accepted. The wedding took place at her father's deathbed, and nine months later a son was born. Mirabel surmises why she allowed herself to be coerced into marrying Arreguí. She loved Manuel but only "up to a point." When he delayed returning, she was not strong enough to resist her father's pressure indefinitely.

The fourth and longest section, "The Battle," takes up the events of the following day. When Manuel sees Soledad at the procession of the "Niño de la Bola," he rushes at her, but Muley averts a confrontation by literally dragging him off. Soledad's mother appears with the baby and makes her second plea. Finally Muley leaves Manuel alone in the church with the statue of the "Niño de la Bola." During the course of a long vigil, he has a change of heart. The next morning he heads out of town, meets Antonio Arreguí, and they salute each other. The novel is apparently going to end peacefully, if not happily.

In the brief epilogue the situation quickly and melodramatically reverses itself. Soledad, no longer able to suppress her love, writes a passionate letter to Manuel. Her perfidious servant, anxious for revenge because Caifás had foreclosed the mortgage on her family's property, gives it to Vitriolo, the ugly, antireligious pharmacist's assistant, who had been spurned by Soledad. Seething with rancor, he sends a messenger after Manuel with the letter. Manuel returns that afternoon while the dance is in progress. He bids a huge sum to dance with Soledad which her husband cannot match. In the embrace which traditionally ends each dance, Manuel, in a moment of frenzied passion, crushes her to death. Arreguí in turn stabs Manuel and kills him. The ill-starred lovers have come to a tragic end.

II *A Romantic Novel*

After *El final de Norma*, *El Niño de la Bola* is the most Romantic of Alarcón's novels. *El escándalo* is first of all a didactic work; the Romantic influence is seen mainly in the fortuitous twists of the plot. In *El Niño de la Bola*, on the contrary, the passionate love story is all important; ideology plays a secondary role. Montesinos went so far as to say: "Our best Romantic novel is possibly *El Niño de la Bola*."[1]

The action takes place in the year 1840 at the height of the Romantic movement. Realizing that the novel hearkened back to an earlier period, Alarcón himself likened it to a drama of that era (p. 614). The situation is similar to that of *Los amantes de Teruel*, and

Alarcón actually mentions Hartzenbusch's drama several times during the course of the novel. In both works the protagonist returns too late and finds the girl he loves married to someone else.

Like the typical Romantic hero, Manuel is predestined to lose the only thing in life he really wants, Soledad. He himself complains of his "unlucky star," which prevents him from achieving happiness (p. 686). He falls in love with Soledad, whose father has caused the ruin of his family. The author himself suggests the parallel with *Romeo and Juliet* and *Lucia di Lammermoor*. (He was, of course, more familiar with Donizetti's opera than with Scott's novel.) Throughout the book Manuel behaves irrationally. He actually speaks to Soledad only once during the course of the novel, and then she does not answer him. They fall in love without really knowing each other. After his father's death, he does not talk for three years. Then he spends three more years living like a savage in the mountains trying to rid himself of his love for Soledad. He is convinced that Soledad will be waiting for him when he returns after eight years, even though no one has heard from him during that interval. And his final act—his crushing Soledad to death—is the handiwork of a demented madman.

Until her final letter Soledad appears as a shadowy, indistinct figure. She does not open her mouth during the course of the whole novel. It is from her mother that Manuel finds out about her interest in him. Alarcón gives no details about the struggle between the father and daughter before her marriage to Arreguí. Only in the epilogue do we discover from her letter that Mirabel's explanation, that she did not love Manuel enough, is faulty. She married Arreguí to avoid being shut up in a cloister where she could never see Manuel again. She beseeches Manuel not to leave, and, although she does not use the term, she seems ready to embark on an adulterous relationship. Her passion turns out to be as wild and uncontrolled as his.

Alarcón's language in the novel is frequently on a level with the unbridled emotions portrayed. He uses three clichés to describe Manuel upon his first appearance: "His glance united at the same time the fearful majesty of the lion, the ferocity of the eagle, and the innocence of the child" (p. 616). There is an incongruous antithesis between the first two metaphors and the third. The passage is reminiscent of *El final de Norma*.[2] Toward the end of the novel, Manuel, thinking he has lost Soledad forever, hyperbolically complains to Muley: "The hurricane of misfortune has enveloped me in its wings" (p. 684). Again the metaphor is more typical of 1840 than of 1880.

III *Ideology*

Although *El Niño de la Bola* is principally a tale of tragic love, Alarcón's conservative ideology also comes through. The title, *El Niño de la Bola,* the traditional representation of the Infant Jesus holding a globe in his hand, implies a religious theme. When left an orphan, Manuel was attracted to the statue. After the three years he spent without talking, the first words he spoke were addressed to it, and the townspeople nicknamed him "El Niño de la Bola." During the years he spent away from Guadix, he lost his faith. Upon returning, he felt no religious or ethical barrier stood between him and Soledad. But then Muley's moral example had its effect, and during the course of his night's vigil alone with the statue, Manuel had a change of heart and resolved to go off. His religious heritage surfaced temporarily until Soledad's letter threw him again into a state of frenzy. Actually, the Infant Jesus and what he represents do not play a very important role in the novel, and the title is not all that appropriate.

Manuel returns home after eight years to find the woman he loves married and a mother to boot. Alarcón could hardly sanction Manuel's continuing to court Soledad, and as his mouthpiece he created Trinidad Muley. In his *Historia de mis libros* he stated that he deliberately chose a good-hearted, uneducated priest to befriend and advise Manuel rather than a worldly and sophisticated Jesuit as in *El escándalo.* A simple parish priest, *un cura de misa y olla* (a priest who says Mass and eats stew), Muley knows no dogma to preach. His advice is human, ethical; it is not exclusively Catholic, or even Christian; it is what a person of any religious belief might give.

Muley even has his ridiculous side—his inordinate obesity—which makes him that much more human. At one point Manuel tries to embrace his mentor: " 'Leave me alone!' cried the voluminous priest, moving away. But Manuel would not let him escape and embraced him in sections" (p. 683). The selfless Muley is among Alarcón's most successful creations. Only one aspect of him seems incongruous. When at the end of the novel he advises Manuel to leave, he tries to console the young man by telling the story of his own life. He had been in love and about to get married when his father died. In order to support his widowed mother and seven younger brothers and sisters he renounced marriage and took holy orders. One wonders how strong his vocation had been.

Vitriolo (Vitriol)—the nickname is well-chosen—is the villain of the novel, who unleashes the tragedy. Bitterly antireligious, he not only wants to gain revenge on Soledad for spurning him, but also to get the better of Muley. Alarcón was afraid of being accused of loading the dice against the liberal cause by making Vitriolo so evil and in the *Historia de mis libros* he emphasizes that another freethinking liberal in the novel, Paco Antúnez, is a very decent person.

In the two other ideological novels, but especially in *El escándalo*, there is little humor. The characters are pretty much of a piece, either all black or all white, and they are not treated ironically. In *El Niño de la Bola* Alarcón pokes fun at the *tertulia* of the liberal Mirabel, whose full name was the pompous-sounding Trajano Pericles de Mirabel y Salmerón. His two given names, the first of a Roman emperor, the second of a Greek statesman, indicated that his father, like so many Spaniards during the reign of Charles III, had felt spiritual ties with the Encyclopedists. Mirabel is a variation of Mirabeau, while Nicolás Salmerón was an educator and politician of that era with Krausist leanings.

In Pepito, the seventeen-year-old poet, Alarcón may well be making fun of some of his own juvenile excesses. Since Pepito was the eighth of twelve boys, his father had been unable to send him away to the university. He had read omnivorously, whatever was available in Guadix, and "he was, at the time, presumed to be the coming man of letters in the province" (p. 657). The verb "presumed" cuts him down to size. He wrote Romantic tragedies in the manner of his idol, Victor Hugo. His dream was to make his name in Madrid. But then Alarcón adds details, which are certainly not autobiographical, to emphasize the ridiculous side of the aspiring poet. He was a homely adolescent, with a big nose and squeaky voice, and he dressed in abominable taste. In religion he was a disciple of Voltaire and in politics of Mirabeau, but he kept these opinions to himself, and no one suspected him of such heresies.

Even more devastating is the portrait of the thirty-year-old Luisa, whom Alarcón alternately calls the *madrileña* and the *forastera* (a person from another part of Spain). The second cousin of a marquis, she has impressed Guadix society by her sophistication and her clothes. At one point she slips the French phrase *C'est ça* (That's it) into the conversation, and the pedantic Mirabel unnecessarily translates it for the rest of the *tertulia*. He is much taken with her and refers to her as a *Diana cazadora* (huntress). His wife, who sees through her, corrects him: "I don't deny that she may be a Diana as regards chastity. . . . But who knows whether she will turn out to be a Diana fisherwoman [*pescadora*]!" (i.e., one who is out for a husband, p. 656). Although Luisa reads antireligious books, she attends Mass regularly and even enjoys the conversation of priests, provided they are learned and well-dressed. Pepito, who fancies himself in love with her, is much impressed by her literary credentials: "She came from the world of which he was always dreaming! She stood in the front line of the court Olympians! She had known Larra, more glorious then for having committed suicide than for having written his immortal works! She was on familiar terms [*tuteaba*] with Espronceda, or Pepe, as this goddess used to call the demigod of those fortunate times! Her portrait had been painted in oils by the Duque de Rivas, the creator of *Don Alvaro o la fuerza del sino*" (p. 658). Alarcón pretends to set Luisa on a pedestal; she is a goddess and can look down on Espronceda, who is only a demigod. Alarcón might well have exercised this satirical gift of his more often in his novels.

These characters are not integral to the main action, and the chapter devoted to them is titled "Two Portraits by Way of an Hors d'Oeuvre." Yet, Luisa, in particular, does perform a function in the novel. Mirabel recounts to his *tertulia* how Soledad came to marry Arreguí, and the romantic *madrileña* is enthralled by this tale of crossed lovers. Later, when Muley prevails upon Manuel to leave, she is disappointed. Such a tranquil ending may be more moral, but it is too prosaic. In similar fashion, the group of travelers in the opening scene and the crowds at the two dances comment on Alarcón's headstrong protagonist and his ill-starred passion. Several times Alarcón uses the term *coro*, chorus, to characterize those peripheral groups whose comments serve to heighten the tension of the novel.

IV *Critical Reception*

Although *El Niño de la Bola* was a popular success and the first edition was sold out within forty-eight hours, the critics almost to a man reacted hostilely. The one exception was Alarcón's friend Alfredo Escobar, who raved in a brief note in *La Epoca* that he had not had time to read the novel, only to devour it.[3]

Revilla treated *El Niño de la Bola* even more harshly than he had *El escándalo*. He granted that in *El Niño de la Bola* Alarcón, who had been so ultramontane in the previous novel, merely defended religious spiritualism, but he still found the thesis objectionable. Although he praised some of the secondary characters, Muley, Caifás, and his wife, he found Manuel's actions illogical and unbelievable and Soledad as shown by her final letter completely reprehensible. He saw that the novel had a good deal in common with Echegaray's melodramas: "If carefully examined, *El Niño de la Bola* is a drama by Echegaray in the form of a novel."[4]

Clarín in an equally adverse review repeated many of the same points. In addition, he strongly objected to Alarcón's portrayal of the so-called liberal characters, Mirabel, Luisa, and especially Vitriolo, whom he found merely a caricature.[5] Alarcón's defense of his novel in the *Historia de mis libros* is largely a rebuttal of these two hostile reviews.

Antonio de Valbuena, notorious for his caustic pen, treated the novel even more severely. He summarized the action at some length, emphasizing with tongue in cheek its inconsistencies, and went so far as to advise people to avoid reading the novel.[6] A review signed T. in the *Revista Contemporánea* was only slightly less unfavorable. Once again the critic praised the lesser figures but found the two protagonists "incomprehensible."[7] Finally a would-be humorist, using the pseudonym Lais, wrote a brief but acerbic and heavy-handed article in the short lived satirical weekly *El Escándalo*. A sample quip: "In town they call Manuel the Infant of the Globe when they might well have called him the Infant of the Pumpkin."[8]

The reception accorded *El Niño de la Bola* upon its first publication was unduly harsh. The major critics, liberal in their orientation, found little good to say about the novel. A decade later the situation had cooled down, and the novel was treated with greater equanimity. Pardo Bazán, who was not unsympathetic to Alarcón's ideological position, viewed the novel more favorably and probably more fairly. She had reservations about it as a didactic novel, but as a Romantic novel she found it admirable.[9] A few years later, Alarcón's friend Valera went so far as to claim that he even preferred *El Niño de la Bola* to *El sombrero de tres picos.*[10]

Almost twenty years later, the novel again came into the limelight. In 1898 Joaquín Dicenta, with the collaboration of Manuel Paso, put on an adaptation of *El Niño de la Bola* as a lyric drama entitled *Curro Vargas* with music by Ruperto Chapí. It turned out to be a big success. Dicenta followed his model quite closely. He changed the title (the protagonist is now called Curro Vargas) and the names of all the characters except for Soledad, and he added farcical scenes for comic relief; but Soledad is the only character who is basically altered. Now she has married of her own free will, humiliated that Curro Vargas's threat upon leaving town had driven all her prospective suitors away. Alarcón's family brought suit against the authors for plagiarism, and a polemic broke out in the press. Valera, Jacinto Octavio Picón, Eugenio Sellés, and Bretón, among others, defended Dicenta, while Echegaray was one of the few on the other side. According to Valera, Dicenta had certainly imitated *El Nino de la Bola,* but Alarcón had done exactly the same thing in *El sombrero de tres picos.*[11]

CHAPTER 11

El Capitán Veneno

E l Capitán Veneno (Captain Poison), which came out in 1881, has little in common with the ideological novels of those years, *El escándalo*, *El Niño de la Bola*, and *La Pródiga*. It is a short, somewhat sentimental love story which is told with engaging humor. It is a reversal of the traditional story of *The Taming of the Shrew*; this time it is the intractable man who is brought to terms.

El Capitán Veneno is the shortest of Alarcón's novels, about three-fourths as long as *El sombrero de tres picos* and almost the same length as "El amigo de la muerte," the longest of the short stories. Some critics have questioned whether *El Capitán Veneno* or even *El sombrero de tres picos* should be called novels rather than short stories.[1] But actually both works are too long and multifaceted to be considered anything but short novels, which is how Alarcón himself classified them.

Like Alarcón's other novels, with the exception of *El sombrero de tres picos*, *El Capitán Veneno* is first divided into books, in this case four sections of approximately equal length, and then into chapters, which, except for the climactic penultimate chapter, are all short. The frequent breaks cause this already short novel to seem to move even more rapidly. It is a compact and tightly focused work with no secondary plots or digressions. There are only six characters and all the action takes place within a period of two months in the same setting, the heroine's apartment near the Puerta del Sol in Madrid.

I *A Novel of Psychological Analysis*

Captain Veneno is not a static character; he changes, mellowing as the novel progresses. Initially he appears as an acerbic and irascible curmudgeon. Gradually, under Angustias's influence, he is transformed into a warmhearted and generous individual and a doting father.

118

The action begins in late March 1848. The republicans have risen up against Isabel II, and skirmishing is going on in the streets of Madrid. The captain, who has been wounded, is carried by Angustias, her mother, and the servant into their house. When he regains consciousness, his initial brusque question fits his nickname, Captain Poison: "Where in the devil am I?" His lifelong aversion to the female sex explodes forth when he finds that he is being cared for by three women: "Women! What the devil!" He does not want to be treated kindly, to owe favors to anyone, and he goes so far as to characterize himself as *un hombre atroz* (an awful, terrifying person). After insulting the servant by referring to her as "that unbearable Galician," he softens the effect by jokingly calling her "beautiful." Angustias, already aware how much pose there is to his misanthropy, quietly smiles, and the mother looks knowingly on (pp. 718–21).

The next morning the doctor sets the broken leg. He, too, sees through the captain and calls him a spoiled child. The captain's cousin, the Marquis of Tomillares, fills the two women in on the patient's background. His mother died in childbirth; his father committed suicide soon afterwards; and he spent his youth in boarding schools. He would have had a brilliant career in the army but for his independence and tactlessness, which were constantly landing him in hot water.

Later that day the captain challenges Angustias to a game of *tute* (a card game). In less than twenty-four hours the impenitent bachelor has fallen for a pair of pretty eyes. Two weeks later the captain is constantly joking with the mother and daughter, referring to Angustias as *Doña Náuseas* and the young princess of Santurce. (Her father had been awarded the title of Count of Santurce by the Carlist pretender Carlos V.) But when, in a moment of pique, he claims that he does not want to play *tute* anymore and the game is discontinued, he is stuck with his decision, for his pride will not allow him to back down. She goes so far as to tell him that his ferocious airs are a false front: ". . . You are a poor fellow with a good heart, which you have chained and gagged up, I don't know whether through pride or through fear of your own sensibility" (p. 731).

One day when Angustias and the servant are at church, the lawyer informs the mother that her petition to be granted a pension has been denied, leaving her penniless. She had been in ill-health for some time and now suffers a heart attack. Late that night, alone with the captain, she asks him to act as Angustias's guardian after her death. Angustias, awakened by the commotion, enters, and she and the captain sorrowfully embrace over the mother's dead body.

Two weeks later on a beautiful May morning the captain and Angustias have their final confrontation, which ends with the complete surrender of the erstwhile intransigent misogynist. A recent letter from her lawyer has made Angustias realize that she is destitute and that the captain has been paying the bills since her mother's death. She tells him that he is now well and must leave and that she is going to work to support herself. The captain makes a series of proposals which she successively rejects. First, he will continue living with her as a boarder. Second, he will support her, although each of them will have his own place. After ten years, when people will no longer make fun of him for succumbing to a woman, they can get married. Finally, he agrees to an immediate marriage but with the preposterous provision that any children they might have be put in a foundling home. Angustias laughingly tells him that they will take the baby there together. The inevitable has occurred, and the captain has been snared. In the final chapter, which takes place four years later, the captain is seen on all fours playing with his two children. A three-year-old is riding on his back, while the younger one is pulling him by the tie and shouting: "Giddap, mule!" (p. 744).

The gradual change in the captain is nicely handled. His boorishness comes to the fore at his first appearance. Then his cousin's account of his early life helps to explain how he got to be that way. At the same time, the captain keeps giving himself away, and the mother and daughter soon realize that his brusque exterior is merely a facade.

Alarcón primarily uses dialogue to develop his characters. Occasionally he drops his role as impersonal narrator and has the captain soliloquize, as when he regrets having quarreled with Angustias and admits to missing their games of *tute*. One chapter (Part III, Chapter II) is written in dialogue form as though it were a play. (He had already used this technique in the 1855 version of *El final de Norma*, but then altered that chapter in the definitive edition of the novel.)

In the concluding chapter Alarcón views the story from a different vantage point. A previously unmentioned character, supposedly the narrator, enters the captain's new home (he has inherited the deceased marquis's title and palace) and finds the former ogre romping with his children. By giving this scene a different focus, the alteration in the captain is made that much more striking. This chapter is titled *"Etiamsi omnes,"* the first part of the quotation, *Etiamsi omnes negaverint te, ego non* (Even when all others deny you, I will not). This is what Peter said to Christ in the Garden of Olives, but soon afterwards he denied Christ three times. Similarly, the captain's fortitude did not hold up. His avowed misogyny quickly evaporated once he met Angustias.

II *Comic Effects*

Alarcón's sentimentality occasionally crops up in *El Capitán Veneno*. The scene at the mother's deathbed is quite in the spirit of the *comédie larmoyante*. At other times the old Romantic bombast creeps in. Early in the novel, after the three women have rescued the wounded captain, the mother objects to Angustias's exposing herself to danger again by going to get a doctor. The daughter retorts: ". . . But, mother, remember that my poor father, your noble and valiant husband, wouldn't have bled to death, as he did, the night after a battle, if some merciful hand had stanched the flow of blood from his wounds" (p. 717).

Alarcón plays up the comic side of his story to avoid the pitfall of excessive sentimentality. The captain is, of course, the main source of humor with his impolitic language in the early part and his ludicrous proposals in the climactic confrontation with Angustias. This scene also has its farcical aspect. The captain gesticulates with his crutches, brandishes one of them about as though it were a rapier, and extends it so that Angustias cannot get by when she tries to leave the room.

Three of the other characters have their comic side. The homely Galician servant, who is deathly afraid when the fighting is going on, offers a contrast to the intrepid Angustias. When the captain tells the mother and daughter that they can go to bed and she will watch over him that first night, she retorts: *¡Yo no me quedo sola con este señor!* . . . *Su genio de demonio póneme el cabello de punta y háceme temblar como una cervata* (I won't stay alone with that man! . . . His devilish temper makes my hair stand on end and makes me tremble like a fawn! p. 721). Her language here matches the captain's. Alarcón even imitates the Galician syntax, the enclitic position of the pronoun *me*. He describes her sleeping, snoring loudly "in the best armchair in the room, with her empty forehead pressed down on her knees, for she hadn't realized the chair had a back specifically designed to support the occiput" (p. 718). The learned, scientific word occiput [*occipucio*] seems incongruous when speaking of the ignorant servant and brings the sentence to an amusing close.

The captain's cousin, the Marquis of Tomillares, methodical and pompous in his speech and dress, serves as a foil for the intemperate and impetuous captain. His high-sounding name, Don Alvaro de Córdoba y Alvarez de Toledo, with the repetition Alvaro-Alvarez, the two *de's*, and the two surnames which are the names of ancient Spanish cities, fits his appearance. He is an archconservative who once delivered to the Senate an oration which lasted three days against those barbaric modern innovations, the railroad and the telegraph. When he first appears, he makes a long-winded and grandiloquent speech summarizing the situation and telling the reader little he did not already know. He then closes with the oratorical flourish: *He dicho* (I have spoken). Alarcón has also made a windbag of the doctor, who exhaustively details the captain's injuries. The mother, who places such stock in the title which the Carlist pretender had given her husband, has her ridiculous side, too, but Alarcón chose not to treat her comically.

At times Alarcón adopts a playful tone. He intrudes in the final paragraph of many of the early chapters with personal comments using a pronoun in the first person. We see him making fun of his own sentimentality and lachrymosity. After the mother tells the marquis that she will not accept payment for taking care of the captain, the two of them burst into tears and the servant follows suit. Alarcón then concludes: ". . . We had better turn the page, lest the readers start weeping like babies [*a moco tendido*] and I am left without an audience to tell my poor story to" (p. 727). The reader is made acutely aware of the author's presence, and, at the same time, the novelist involves him in the story.

In his *Historia de mis libros* Alarcón maintained that, like *El sombrero de tres picos*, *El Capitán Veneno* was well received, and, perhaps for that reason, he felt less affection for it than for his more ambitious novels, *El escándalo* and *El Niño de la Bola*, which had been savaged by the critics. His statement about the novel's favorable reception is a little surprising. His friends no doubt praised it to him, but the press virtually neglected it. The only review I found is one by Tomás Tuero in *La Iberia*, which disparagingly dismissed the work as *baladí* (trivial), much inferior to the two previous novels.[2] Clarín, who reviewed most of the novels of any stature which appeared during those years, apparently never mentioned it, nor did Pardo Bazán. The novel was evidently not taken very seriously.

El Capitán Veneno is a minor work. It lacks the color and the varied texture of *El sombrero de tres picos*. Its humor depends too much on the basic situation—woman meets recalcitrant male and tames him. But, within its limitations, it has considerable charm. It is less significant, but, in ways, it wears better than his longer, more pretentious novels.

CHAPTER 12

La Pródiga

I Theme and Structure

THE woman of easy virtue seen from differing vantage points, is a recurring theme in European literature of the second half of the nineteenth century. The younger Dumas's *La Dame aux Camélias* (1852) and Verdi's opera *La Traviata,* which was based on it, present the fallen woman redeemed by love, a completely Romantic conception. The Goncourt brothers initiated the Naturalistic treatment of the theme with *Germinie Lacerteux* (1865), in which a downtrodden servant is exploited by a series of men. In the opposite vein, Zola's infamous *Naná* (1882) destroys all her lovers. Isidora Rufete in Galdós's *La desheredada* (1881) is a victim of her illusions of grandeur and ends up as a prostitute, while the protagonist of Daudet's *Sapho* (1884) abandons her lover after ruining his life. *La Pródiga* (The Prodigal Woman) has a good deal in common with Valera's *Genio y figura,* which appeared fifteen years later. Valera's protagonist is nicknamed Rafaela *la generosa*, although her generosity is different from La Pródiga's. Rafaela has difficulty refusing her admirers, in large part because she likes to give them pleasure. Both characters end up committing suicide, but whereas La Pródiga does so unselfishly to spare her lover unhappiness, Rafaela is motivated by disillusionment with her past life and fear of impending old age.

It is somewhat surprising that Alarcón, who was so opposed to the Naturalistic approach to literature and who was squeamish about sex (witness his violent denunciation of Feydeau's *Fanny*), should have written *La Pródiga* at all. He does treat the potentially erotic theme with discretion, and the novel incurred no adverse criticism along those lines.

Alarcón claims in his *Historia de mis libros* to have written *La*

124

Pródiga within a period of a month during the fall of 1881, just meeting his deadlines as the installments came out in the *Revista Hispano-Americana*. He made a certain number of alterations in the text before publishing the novel in book form early the following year.[1]

La Pródiga opens with the twenty-six-year-old Guillermo de Loja and his two friends, who are campaigning for the Cortes, arriving at a remote *cortijo* (an Andalusian country estate). They find that it is inhabited by Julia, a beautiful thirty-seven-year-old woman with a notorious past. Guillermo falls in love with her at first sight and returns that evening without his friends. She resists his advances, saying that she is too old, that he would soon tire of her, and that his career would be ruined if he married or even lived with her.

Returning to Madrid, Guillermo becomes engrossed with his burgeoning political career. Attracted by Pura, the young and beautiful daughter of a marquis, he virtually forgets Julia. But when he is not given the political position he had hoped for and when he hears that Pura is marrying a wealthy but doddering septuagenarian noble to refurbish the family's fortune, the disillusioned Guillermo hastens back to Julia. Saying that fate has willed it, she no longer resists him but does swear that she will never allow herself to become a burden: "I, the Prodigal Woman, take God as witness that I will not cause you a single day's regret, that you will not hate me for a single hour, that I will not stand in the way of your glory and happiness a single·instant" (p. 795). She vows that when he tires of her and is ready to return to Madrid, she will, in fact, urge him to leave. In the fourth section, "The Four Seasons" (the novel is divided into five books of unequal length), as the year passes and winter approaches, Julia's original prediction becomes increasingly true. Guillermo has trouble keeping occupied; the peasants show their disapproval of the couple's conduct; and the local priest openly rebukes them. Then, in the final section, "The First of October," the anniversary of their first meeting, the pace accelerates, and the story moves quickly toward its tragic climax. Early the next morning Julia commits suicide by drowning herself.

La Pródiga is the most tightly constructed of Alarcón's three ideological novels. There are fewer characters and none is superfluous. The action takes place within a period of a year and moves quickly to the final resolution with no abrupt melodramatic reversals in the action. The didactic bias is also less pronounced than in *El escándalo* or even *El Niño de la Bola*. *La Pródiga* is psychologically a more intuitive novel.

II   *Characterization*

Guillermo de Loja, engineer, lawyer, artist, and politician, is a talented young man with a promising future. Unlike his friends Enrique and Miguel, he is an idealist. He is revolted by the ruthless behavior of other politicians and the false standards of Madrid society. And yet Madrid is his life. He could not be happy for long elsewhere. After being elected deputy, flushed with success and attracted to Pura, he seems to have forgotten his earlier infatuation. He is aware that marrying into the nobility would advance his career. His motives are not unmixed. Then, when his disillusionment causes him to return to Julia, he tries to make a complete break with his past life. He even refuses to read the Madrid paper, and the copies pile up in their wrappers. But he has trouble adjusting to the simple rural life. He seeks to keep busy. Julia perceives that he has an aversion to solitude. He wants to be liked and is hurt when his efforts to ingratiate himself with the peasants are rebuffed. On the final day, the first of October, his unhappiness becomes increasingly apparent. The persistent rain, which keeps them indoors, forecasts the approaching dreary winter. The priest refuses to allow them to serve as sponsors at the wedding of the overseer's son, José. Guillermo peevishly inquires about Julia's previous lovers, and they quarrel. Hearing the noisy wedding festivities going on nearby, Guillermo nastily comments, "How those animals frolic about! What an uproar they make so that the world will be aware that a virgin has ceased to be one! How vain and foolish this biped who was born without feathers is and will continue to be until the end of the world!" (p. 819). When Julia says the time has come for him to leave her and he answers, "I am incapable of committing the infamy of abandoning you" (p. 822), she realizes that she must act. That night, after retiring to her room, she looks through the keyhole and sees him voraciously reading through the pile of old newspapers.

The next day he is, of course, badly shaken up by her suicide, but in the epilogue we see that he makes a full recovery. Some years later he is happily married and a successful politician in Madrid. Ironically, it is Guillermo, the ambivalent lover, who comes out of it unscathed, while La Pródiga, who loved completely and unselfishly, commits suicide in order not to ruin his life.

Baquero Goyanes perceptively compares *La Pródiga* with Benjamin Constant's early psychological novel, *Adolphe* (1816). The situation is similar in the two novels, but Baquero plays down the psychological aspects of Guillermo's increasing boredom and dissatisfaction on the *cortijo* and diagnoses his and Julia's problem as basically ethical and social.[2] Actually, the two factors carry almost equal weight in causing his unhappiness.

Whereas Guillermo is ambitious with basically bourgeois values, Julia is a romantic, ready to sacrifice everything for the man she loves. At first we see her as a woman with an enigmatic past. Only when the novel is a third over does the Count of the Acacias, an old friend of hers, give Guillermo a rundown on her earlier life. He likens her to George Sand's and Byron's heroines. She herself admits that man is her nemesis: "My constant enemy, my doom" (p. 758). When hardly more than a girl, at the instigation of her brother, who also ended up a suicide, she married a brave but uncouth French general, and the marriage ended in divorce. She then embarked on a series of ill-fated love affairs. The Russian prince was killed in a sleighing accident; the Andalusian marquis was the victim of a duel in Trieste; the Spanish minister died insane in Egypt. The Italian tenor bled her of money, before she sent him packing. A Cretan prince fighting for the independence of Greece blew out his brains because he was going to be separated from her. The last was a German duke who wanted her to live quietly with him on his estate after they had both lost their fortunes gambling in Baden-Baden. She refused and returned to her *cortijo*, where she had been living quietly for three years, beloved by the peasants, when Guillermo first entered her life. The count maintained that with money she could have set herself up in Madrid and faced down society; without it, it was impossible. After the flamboyant life she had led for over a decade with her string of international lovers, she readily adjusted to the quiet isolation of the *cortijo*. But then, when another attractive man arrives, she forgets the old wounds and opens her heart to love once more. Again she flaunts conventions. In spite of her irregular love life, the usually straitlaced Alarcón obviously sympathizes with his heroine. An open and unselfish person, there is nothing hypocritical about her. She does what she wants, but she is prepared to pay the price. When she realizes that Guillermo has tired of their idyll, she does not hesitate to break it off.

Her suicide is, of course, a crime in the eyes of the Church. She rationalizes her act, while thinking to herself, as she waits for dawn to break that final morning. Her father was a follower of Voltaire. Brought up in a freethinking atmosphere, she herself had never been a believer. Consequently, she was not bound by Catholic dogma and was free to take her own life.

The other characters in the novel fit into two groups—the *madrileños* and the peasants on the *cortijo*. The former, politicians and members of the upper social stratum, are portrayed as ambitious *arrivistes*. Of Guillermo's two friends, Enrique is obsequious and Miguel is cynical. The ministry Guillermo desired was given to an incompetent party hack for political reasons. The Count of the Acacias is satirically portrayed as the aging man-about-town: "The Count of the Acacias, an adorable man, at least for salon life, without will, personal enthusiasm, or spiritual incentives other than an intelligence as cool and clear as water; all eyes, bald head, exclamations, and smiles. Without passions of his own, he was profoundly disdainful of those of others, and yet he schemed to help his friends get what they wanted. He wore a frock coat the way veteran soldiers wear their uniform. The advancing years did not make him look like an old man so much as a wasted dandy" (p. 776). At the same time, he is one of the few *madrileños* who understood and appreciated Julia.

Pura is the complete antithesis of Julia, and her name is transparently ironical. "A light-complected brunette, a little pale . . . not short, although neither as tall nor as much of a woman as La Pródiga; in appearance slender, but in reality well-built and voluptuous, for she somehow managed to keep her youthful perfections hypocritically and chastely hidden; equally dissembling as far as her character is concerned, for the romantic melancholy of her face served as a mask for a certain joking playfulness most clearly seen in her roguish and charming smiles" (p. 773). The terms "in appearance," "in reality," "hypocritically," "dissembling," and "mask" suggest the duplicity of her character. Pura goes off to Paris to buy her trousseau. Within a few months her husband dies. Her mourning is soon put aside, and she is entertaining on a grand scale. Thanks to her, Enrique later on becomes minister ahead of the more able Guillermo.

Two of the villagers, who, significantly, are not peasants, have much in common with the *madrileños*. The servile secretary, whom everybody dislikes, toadies up to the three candidates, angling for a sinecure in Madrid. At the same time, he is intolerantly critical of Julia behind her back. The priest could hardly be expected to countenance Guillermo and Julia's conduct, but he goes out of his way to make their life difficult, attacking them openly in a sermon and inciting the villagers against them. His hypocrisy comes out in the letter he sends Julia shortly after Guillermo arrives at the *cortijo*, asking her to attend Mass and to set an example for the unfortunate parishioners, whose only consolation is religion. He was apparently little concerned with what Julia and Guillermo really believed as long as they furthered his purposes. Actually, he is the only unsympathetic priest found in Alarcón's fiction.

The simple, virtuous peasants offer a marked contrast to this first group. They are devoted to Julia because of her generosity and kindness and overlook her past transgressions until she openly starts living with Guillermo. *Tío* Antonio, the overseer, although he disapproves of her conduct, is so loyal that he never criticizes her. He chastises his son, José, for showing lack of respect to Guillermo, and it is he who protects Guillermo from the wrath of the villagers after Julia's death and helps him get away. His wife, less tolerant, feigns illness so as not to have to serve Julia. But it is José who reacts the most strongly. Half her age, he idealizes her but at the same time is sensually attracted to her. He describes his reaction when carrying her down a broken stairway: "Upon seeing myself lord and master of such a divine beauty, although it was only for a moment, and upon hearing her joyful laughter by my head, I felt something . . . , as though I were about to die of pleasure and happiness" (p. 755). When he finds her body in the pond, he carries her back to the *cortijo* as though she were his. If Guillermo had married Julia, José would have accepted it. As it is, he feels that the woman he reveres is being defiled. When Guillermo leaves the *cortijo* the final morning, José shoots at him and misses. Guillermo tells him to shoot again, but he turns and disappears, at least pardoning Guillermo his life. The peasants, and José in particular, serve as the "chorus" in this novel to echo Alarcón's views. Our moralist could not condone conduct as flagrantly unconventional as Guillermo and Julia's.

Actually, José and *tío* Antonio are the least convincing characters in the book. In his effort to underline their virtue, Alarcón often pushes them into bathos. When Julia urges José to hurry up and marry his *novia*, he gives as an excuse: "Because . . . , because . . . , if I get married and have children and worries of my own to think about, I will be farther away from your ladyship; I won't be able to live exclusively to serve her; nor will it be so easy for me to die defending her, if need be. I would like to be always looking at my lady, hearing her speak, doing my utmost to please her!" (p. 789). Similarly, Antonio's tone when thanking Julia after the wedding is positively saccharine: "Your ladyship is a saint as always! Allow me to kiss your hand again, and excuse this poor old man's tears which are staining it!" (p. 818).

In his *Historia de mis libros* Alarcón complained that although *La Pródiga* had been a popular success, the critics had formed a cabal and had ignored it. In June his friend Luis Alfonso praised the novel in the *Revista Hispano-Americana*. As this was the journal in which the novel had originally appeared, he could hardly have done otherwise. Alfonso ranked it above *El escándalo* and *El Niño de la Bola:* "*La Pródiga* is the novel which has aroused least comment; intrinsically, however, it is the best of the three."[3] Servando Ruiz Gómez also reviewed the novel favorably in the *Revista de España*, although he did little more than summarize the plot at considerable length.[4] Clarín finally got around to writing about the novel, publishing a brief and hostile note in *La Diana* in October. He found little to praise in the novel: Alarcón's characterization of Julia, Guillermo's soul-searching in Madrid when he is debating between Julia and Pura. Otherwise, he objected to the extravagant plot, the false characterization, and the unnatural dialogue. He concluded with an oblique compliment: "In short, *La Pródiga* is one of Alarcón's worst novels; and, yet, it shows him to be one of our best novelists."[5] After the harsh reception accorded *El Niño de la Bola* two years before, Alarcón was discouraged by this relative neglect. He gave up fiction, and, in fact, wrote little at all during the last decade of his life.

CHAPTER 13

Conclusion

ALTHOUGH Alarcón, born in 1833, was nine years younger than Valera, the two of them came on the literary scene almost at the same time. Valera had published a few poems earlier in periodicals, but he did not start writing prose (mostly literary criticism) until after his return from Río de Janeiro in 1853. Alarcón's youthful stories and sketches, which he published in *El Eco de Occidente* in Cádiz and Granada in 1852–54, passed almost unnoticed. Only after coming to Madrid late in 1854 did he begin to make a name for himself. During the next few years he contributed extensively to the Madrid press material of all sorts—his early novel *El final de Norma*, short stories, sketches, literary criticism, even social notes.

By 1850 Spain had emerged from the throes of Romanticism. There were new currents in the air. Already in the 1840s La Avellaneda had written psychological novels with social overtones such as *Sab* and *Dos mujeres*. In Pastor Díaz's slow-moving *De Villahermosa a la China* (1858) there is even greater emphasis on psychological development. López de Ayala and Tamayo y Baus were beginning to study the problems of contemporary Spanish society in their theater, and there is a new prosaic and ironic note to Campoamor's poetry.

Alarcón is a transitional figure. He was younger than all the above-mentioned writers, but he was by temperament romantically inclined, and the melodramatic element is strong in many of his early works, particularly *El final de Norma* and such *Historietas nacionales* as "El carbonero alcalde," "El afrancesado," "El extranjero," "El ángel de la Guarda," and "¡Buena pesca!" Actually, he never outgrew these Romantic propensities. Even in the late novels, *El escándalo* and *El Niño de la Bola*, the action keeps shifting melodramatically back and forth, and he frequently soars

131

into bombastic flights of language. Of the novelists of his generation, Alarcón was the one with the closest ties to Romanticism.

At the same time, Alarcón believed that didacticism should play an important role in literature. It dominates his early play, *El hijo pródigo*, and is the central theme of his academy discourse, "La moral en el arte." Among the novelists, Alarcón, along with Pereda, was the leader of the conservative, ultramontane forces in their campaign against the liberals, Galdós, Valera, and Clarín. *El escándalo* and, to a lesser extent, *El Niño de la Bola* and *La Pródiga* were Alarcón's answer to Galdós's *Gloria* and Valera's *Pepita Jiménez*.

There is another, more attractive side to Alarcón; he was also a light-hearted, gay Andalusian with a delightful sense of the comic. *El sombrero de tres picos* is justly celebrated. *El Capitán Veneno* trails behind, although it, too, has its charm, and the same can be said of a good many of the short stories, "El libro talonario," "Tic . . . tac," and "La última calaverada." Alarcón also had a gift for social satire, as can be seen in portions of *El Niño de la Bola* and *La Pródiga*. He usually kept it under wraps. It is perhaps unfortunate that he did not exercise this talent more often.

For most people it is one book, *El sombrero de tres picos*, which keeps Alarcón's reputation alive. Certainly it is his masterpiece, but other works of his are read: witness the numerous editions of his novels and short stories which have appeared in recent years. *El escándalo*, *El Niño de la Bola*, and *La Pródiga* have their faults, mainly the result of carry-over from his Romantic heritage, but they still read easily. The reader is swept along by the narrative. They have more than an historical interest as examples of the conservative forces in the ideological struggle of those years. Alarcón's production as a writer of short stories is uneven, ranging from the masterly "La Comendadora," to amusing comic tales, the ultrapatriotic *Historietas nacionales* dealing with the War of Independence, which understandably have been perhaps overpraised by Spaniards, down to such melodramatic tales as "El clavo." There is an even greater range among the sketches, but the best of them, "Un maestro de antaño" and "La Nochebuena del poeta," rank high. Of his travel pieces, *La Alpujarra* and, to a lesser extent, *De Madrid a Nápoles* are of interest to the modern reader, while his *Diario de un testigo de la Guerra de Africa* offers a vivid, if somewhat biased, account of the war. The rest of his writing—*El final de Norma*, *El hijo pródigo*, virtually all the poetry, much of the literary criticism, most of the shorter travel pieces, the weaker stories and sketches—can be pretty much forgotten. But an appreciable amount of what Alarcón wrote holds up today. It has something to say to the contemporary reader.

Where does Alarcón stand today among his contemporaries? Certainly his reputation depends in good part on *El sombrero de tres picos*. One might say that it is a *minor* masterpiece, because it is a short, comic tale with no deeper implications. In spite of its charm, it lacks the depth and breadth of Galdós's great novels or of Clarín's *La Regenta*. Valera has always been ranked ahead of Alarcón. *Pepita Jiménez* is, no doubt, a more subtle, more sophisticated novel than *El sombrero de tres picos*, and Valera's novelistic production as a whole is superior to Alarcón's. He also surpasses Alarcón as a critic and thinker. Different as the two novels are, one could justifiably say that *El sombrero de tres picos* holds its own with *Los pazos de Ulloa*, but again, as is the case with Valera, Alarcón cannot match the breadth and scope of Pardo Bazán's work. She exerted a powerful leavening force on Spanish literature and thought for over three decades. Compared with her, Alarcón was a timid parochial. Pereda is a special case. Fifty years ago he was generally considered the number-two novelist of his generation, second only to Galdós. Today his reputation has waned. At best he is an awkward novelist. *Sotileza* has a simplistic and contrived plot, but it also contains masterful scenes in which he vividly describes the harsh life of the fishermen. The *costumbrista* elements, along with the epic descriptions of nature, are the strongest parts of his novels. At his best, and he is frequently at his best, Pereda has a power which Alarcón never attains. In the last two decades of the nineteenth century Palacio Valdés was the Spanish novelist most widely translated in the United States. He was a particular favorite of William Dean Howells. His star has faded, too, and today his novels seem old-fashioned and a little colorless, and Alarcón should be ranked ahead of him. All these novelists owe a debt of gratitude to Fernán Caballero for breaking trail and getting the Spanish novel off on a new tack, but her importance today is largely historical. Her novels date badly, and they read with difficulty.

The Spanish novelists of the second half of the nineteenth century might well be ranked in the following order: Galdós, Clarín, Valera, Pardo Bazán, Pereda, Alarcón, Palacio Valdés, and Fernán Caballero. That puts Alarcón in sixth place, which is not bad.

Notes and References

Chapter One

1. Quoted by Julio Romano, *Pedro Antonio de Alarcón* (Madrid, 1933), pp. 38–40.

2. Luis Martínez Kleiser, *Don Pedro Antonio de Alarcón* reprinted as an introduction to Alarcón, *Obras completas* (Fax), p. vi.

3. Alarcón says he published it when he was seventeen or eighteen (p. 9). But where? It came out later, no doubt in a revised version, in the *Museo Universal* in 1857.

4. See Manuel León Sánchez and José Cascales Muñoz, *Antología de la Cuerda granadina* (Mexico, 1928).

5. J. Calvo y Teruel, "Biografía de don Pedro Antonio de Alarcón," in Alarcón, *Poesías serias y humorísticas* (Madrid, 1870), p. xiii.

6. E. Herman Hespelt has thoroughly analyzed Alarcón's association with *El Látigo* and his contributions to it in "Alarcón as Editor of *El Látigo,*" *Hispania*, XIX (1936), 319–36. Barnett A. McClendon goes over much of the same ground in "Political and Moral Evolution of Pedro Antonio de Alarcón," *Dos Continentes*, IX–X (1971–72), 13–25, although he plays down Alarcón's liberalism and anticlericalism.

7. The article, "Alarcón *(Ultimos escritos),*" originally appeared in *Madrid Cómico* and was reprinted in *Palique* (Madrid, 1893), pp. 289–93.

8. *Retratos y apuntes literarios* (Madrid, n.d.), p. 153.

Chapter Two

1. For Byron and Alarcón see José F. Montesinos, *Pedro Antonio de Alarcón* (Zaragoza, 1955), pp. 13–15.

2. "La portera de Victor Hugo," *La Ilustración*, VII (1855), 487.

3. *La Ilustración*, VIII (1856), 11.

4. See Montesinos, "Notas sueltas sobre la fortuna de Balzac en España," *Revue de Littérature Comparée*, XXIV (1950), 309–38.

5. Alarcón is also supposed to have written for *El Criterio* in 1857, but neither the Biblioteca Nacional nor the Hemeroteca Municipal in Madrid has copies of the paper for that year.

6. *La Discusión,* May 25 and July 22, 1856.

7. *La Discusión,* July 22, 1856, and April 11, 1858.

8. *O.C.,* pp. 1785–88; *La Epoca,* Jan. 22, 1859.

9. *La Discusión,* June 29, July 6, 13, and 22, 1856. There was to have been a fifth article on the novels, but either the article was never published or that particular issue is missing from the Hemeroteca Municipal.

10. *La Discusión,* July 24, 1858. The article was reprinted in the first edition of *Cosas que fueron* (1871) but was not collected in *O.C.*

11. See Montesinos, "Sobre *El escándalo* de Alarcón," in *Ensayos y estudios de literatura española* (Mexico, 1959), pp. 178–87.

12. See John Eugene Englekirk, *Edgar Allan Poe in Hispanic Literature* (New York, 1934), pp. 56–61.

13. Manuel de la Revilla, "Revista crítica," *Revista Contemporánea,* VIII (1877), 121–24.

14. "Verdades como puños," *El Solfeo,* no. 502, March 5, 1877, and no. 513, March 14, 1877, reprinted in *Preludios de "Clarín,"* ed. Jean François Botrel (Oviedo, 1972), pp. 111–15.

15. *Preludios de "Clarín,"* p. 111.

16. *La Discusión,* Nov. 26, 1858.

17. "Contra las zarzuelas," an article extracted from reviews originally published in 1858 and 1859, was reprinted in *Juicios literarios y artísticos* (*O.C.,* pp. 1817–24).

18. The 1858 articles were collected in part in *Juicios literarios y artísticos* (*O.C.,* pp. 1808–13). For a summary of these and extracts of the contents of others, see Enrique Pardo Canalis, "Alarcón y las bellas artes," *Revista de Ideas Estéticas,* XVI (1958), 291–310.

Chapter Three

1. Although they were collected and advertised for sale in a bound volume, neither the various Madrid libraries, the municipal *hemerotecas* (periodical libraries) of Granada, Cádiz, or Seville, the university libraries in Granada or Seville, nor the Biblioteca de Temas Gaditanos in Cádiz has a copy of it.

2. The Biblioteca Nacional has a copy; the Biblioteca Central of the University of Granada, two; and the Hemeroteca Municipal in Granada, a broken file.

3. In 1926 Aguilar published a second edition of the work under a new title, *Verdades de paño pardo y otros escritos olvidados,* omitting the poetry and altering the order of the other pieces.

4. *Cuentos, artículos y novelas,* 2nd, 3rd, and 4th series (Madrid, 1859).

5. *Novelas* (Madrid, 1866). This volume has escaped the notice of recent critics. Neither Simón Díaz nor Montesinos mentions it. There is a copy in the Library of Congress. It contains "El amigo de la muerte," "El coro de ángeles," "¿Por qué era rubia?", "El clavo," "Soy, tengo y quiero," "Los

seis velos," "El abrazo de Vergara," "Fin de una novela," "El carbonero alcalde," "¡Viva el Papa!", "Las dos glorias," "La corneta de llaves," "¡Buena pesca!", "Mañanas de abril y mayo," "La buenaventura," and "El año en Spitzberg." A second edition, *Novelas* (Madrid, n.d. [1872]), contains an additional story, "Novela natural."

6. "Revista de España," *El Periódico Ilustrado*, II (May 27, 1866), 130.

7. The prose pieces from *Amores y amoríos* which eventually were kept in the *Obras completas* include "Sinfonía—Conjugación del verbo amar," "Lo que se oye desde una silla del Prado," "La Comendadora," "Sin un cuarto," "Tic . . . tac," "La última calaverada," the sketch "La granadina," and the travel article "Una visita al Monasterio de Yuste."

8. Montesinos, *Pedro Antonio de Alarcón*, pp. 90–91.

9. A. H. Krappe, "The Source of Pedro Antonio de Alarcón's 'El afrancesado,' " *Romanic Review*, XVI (1925), 54–56.

10. W. L. Fichter, "El carácter tradicional de 'El afrancesado' de Alarcón," *Revista de Filología Hispánica*, VII (1945), 162–63.

11. A. H. Krappe in "The Source of Pedro Antonio de Alarcón's 'El extranjero,' " *Hispanic Review*, II (1943), 72–76, rather unconvincingly argues that the source of Alarcón's story is a Yugoslav ballad, which Alarcón presumably read in a French translation. The similarities between the ballad and Alarcón's story are slight. As in the case of "El afrancesado," it seems more likely that Alarcón is simply retelling a popular tale which circulated in Spain during the years following the Napoleonic invasion.

12. Pardo Bazán, *Retratos y apuntes literarios*, p. 171.

13. Montesinos, *Pedro Antonio de Alarcón*, p. 113.

14. *El Mundo Pintoresco*, I (1858), 235–38, 243–44, 254–55, 258–59.

15. Ibid., p. 255.

16. Alarcón, *Dos ángeles caídos y otros escritos olvidados* (Madrid, 1924), p. 18.

17. Alarcón, *Novelas*, 2nd ed. (Madrid, [1872]), p. 367.

18. Montesinos, *Pedro Antonio de Alarcón*, p. 118.

19. Ibid., p. 120.

20. *O.C.*, p. 9. *Crispino e la comàre* with music by Luigi Ricci and libretto by Piave was first performed in Venice in 1850. Pedro Antonio de Alarcón, *La Comendadora y otros cuentos*, ed. Laura de los Ríos (Madrid, 1975), pp. 87–88. See also Montesinos, *Pedro Antonio de Alarcón*, p. 44, and Mariano Baquero Goyanes, *El cuento español en el siglo XIX* (Madrid, 1949), p. 244.

Chapter Four

1. First published in *El Museo Universal* in 1858, it was collected in *Historietas nacionales* rather than *Cosas que fueron*.

2. It first appeared in *El Eco de Occidente* in 1854 and was collected in *Dos ángeles caídos y otros escritos olvidados*.

3. "Las ferias de Madrid" first appeared in *La Discusión* in 1858 and was republished in *Cosas que fueron*.

4. After appearing in *El Museo Universal*, III (1859), 2, "Madrid a vista de buho" was never collected in *O.C.*

5. *Dos ángeles caídos*, p. 70.

6. The sketch was collected in *Viajes por España* rather than in *Cosas que fueron*.

7. Both "El año campesino" and "Mayo" were collected in *Historietas nacionales*.

8. It was collected in *Ultimos escritos*.

9. Alarcón's article was later collected in *Ultimos escritos*.

10. Surprisingly enough, it was collected in *Narraciones inverosímiles* rather than *Cosas que fueron*.

11. See José F. Montesinos, *Costumbrismo y novela. Ensayo sobre el redescubrimiento de la realidad española* (Berkeley, 1960), pp. 95–106.

12. "La fea" was reprinted in *La Ilustracion*, VII (1855), 167, 175, in *Cosas que fueron*, and in *O.C.*, pp. 1702–15, while "La hermosa" was collected in *Dos ángeles caídos*.

13. *Dos ángeles caídos*, p. 56.

Chapter Five

1. "Viaje a París in 1855" was never republished. The other articles were collected, usually in a shortened version, in *Viajes por España*.

2. These articles first appeared in *La Ilustración Española y Americana* and were then collected in *Ultimos escritos*.

3. *La Epoca*, July 18, 1860.

4. Benito Pérez Galdós, *Obras completas*, III (Madrid, 1951), p. 257.

5. Anonymous reviews appeared in *La España*, Feb. 26, 1862, and *La Discusión*, March 4, 1862. Ramón de Mesonero Romanos, "Crítica literaria," *La Ilustración Española y Americana*, XXV:1 (1881), 6–7.

Chapter Six

1. "Pedro Antonio de Alarcón," *Nuevo Teatro Crítico*, II (Jan. 1892), 49.

2. *Las Cortes*, Nov. 9, 1857.

3. "Revista de teatros. *El hijo pródigo* de don Pedro Antonio de Alarcón," *La Iberia*, Nov. 6, 1857. "Revista dramática," *El Estado*, Nov. 17, 1857.

Chapter Seven

1. I was unable to locate a copy of the rare first (1855) edition of *El final de Norma*, but I was able to read this early version of the novel in the *feuilletons* of *El Occidente* and *La Epoca*. See my article, "A Variant Study of Alarcón's *El final de Norma*," to appear in a homage volume dedicated to Gerald E. Wade.

2. *El sombrero. Su pasado, su presente y su porvenir* (Madrid, 1859), p. 102.

3. *Pedro Antonio de Alarcón*, p. 143.

Chapter Eight

1. Alarcón's remarks about the genesis of the novel are found in the Preface published in the *Revista Europea* and in the first edition of 1874. The last part of the Preface, including the references to Villanueva and Zorrilla, was eliminated from the later editions of the novel. Martínez Kleiser gives additional data on the genesis of the novel, quoting from Alarcón's correspondence with Zorrilla and others (*O.C.*, p. xxii).

2. Adolfo Bonilla y San Martín, "Los orígenes de *El sombrero de tres picos*," *Revue Hispanique*, XIII (1905), 5–17. Bonilla claims that Boccaccio's tale is in the tradition of the exemplary tale, "The Story of the Master and the Manservant, of the Wife and the Husband, and How They All Found Themselves Together," from *El libro de los engaños* (The Book of the Wiles of Women), which Prince Fadrique, brother of Alfonso *el Sabio*, had translated from Arabic into Spanish in the thirteenth century, but, outside of being a story of adultery, it bears slight resemblance to the Italian tale and has almost nothing in common with *El sombrero de tres picos*.

3. R. Foulché-Delbosc, "D'où dérive *El sombrero de tres picos*," *Revue Hispanique*, XVIII (1908), 468–87.

4. Joseph E. Gillet, "A New Analogue of Alarcón's *El sombrero de tres picos*," *Revue Hispanique*, LXXIII (1928), 616–28.

5. Edwin B. Place, "The Antecedents of *El sombrero de tres picos*," *Philological Quarterly*, VIII (1929), 39–42.

6. J. A. van Praag, "Un precursor holandés de 'El Molinero de Arcos,'" *Clavileño*, IV, no. 19 (1953), 7–9.

7. Samuel G. Armistead and Joseph H. Silverman, "'El Corregidor y la Molinera': Some Unnoticed Germanic Antecedents," *Philological Quarterly*, LI (1972), 279–91.

8. Edmund De Chasca discusses Alarcón's treatment of the "honor" theme in his perceptive article, "La forma cómica en *El sombrero de tres picos*," *Hispania*, XXXVI (1953), 283–88.

9. Manuel de Góngora, "Cartas literarias," *Revista Europea*, VII (1876), 153–59.

10. See De Chasca, p. 287.

11. In later editions of the novel Alarcón made only a limited number of minor changes in the text, usually for the better, as here. Arcadio López-Casanova has indicated the variants in his edition of *El sombrero de tres picos* (Madrid, 1974).

12. See De Chasca, p. 286.

13. Ibid., p. 287.

14. *El sombrero de tres picos*, ed. Arcadio López-Casanova, pp. 46–47.

15. I have not been able to locate where Alfonso's review first appeared. It was reprinted in 1882 as an Introduction to the "Colección de Escritores Castellanos" edition of the novel and again in *O.C.*, pp. 441–43.

16. Manuel de la Revilla, "Bocetos literarios. D. Pedro Antonio de Alarcón," *Revista Contemporánea*, XI (1877), 17–26; reprinted in *Obras* (Madrid, 1883), p. 95.

17. Armando Palacio Valdés, "Los novelistas españoles. Don Pedro Antonio de Alarcón," *Revista Europea*, XI (1878), 465–69.

18. Emilia Pardo Bazán, *Retratos y apuntes literarios*, p. 182.

19. Juan Valera, *Obras completas*, II (Madrid, 1961), 1364.

20. José F. Montesinos, *Pedro Antonio de Alarcón*, p. 156. Ricardo Gullón, "Alarcón, el romántico," *Insula*, no. 120 (Dec. 1955), 1, 3, 4. Vicente Gaos, "Técnica y estilo de *El sombrero de tres picos*," in *Temas y problemas de literatura española* (Madrid, 1959), pp. 179–201.

Chapter Nine

1. See Francisco Pérez Gutiérrez, *El problema religioso en la generación de 1868* (Madrid, 1975), especially pp. 97–129.

2. *El escándalo*, ed. Mariano Baquero Goyanes, "Clásicos Castellanos" (Madrid, 1973), I, 81; II, 51, 169.

3. "Allegory in *El escándalo*," *Modern Language Notes*, LXXXVII (1972), 324–29.

4. *O.C.*, pp. 504, 507, 554, 557, 563, 599, 603, 606.

5. "Alarcón in *El escándalo*," *Modern Language Notes*, LXXXIII (1968), 212–25.

6. *Retratos y apuntes literarios*, p. 132.

7. D. Gamallo Fierros, "*El escándalo* fue inspirado por Pastor Díaz, moribundo," *Ya*, Oct. 22, 23, 26, 1943. Gamallo Fierros, "Sigue *El escándalo*," *El Español*, II, no. 55 (Nov. 13, 1943), 1, 12. Luis Martínez Kleiser, "Sobre *El escándalo*," *Ya*, Oct. 23, 1943.

8. José F. Montesinos, "Sobre *El escándalo* de Alarcón," in *Ensayos y estudios de literatura española*, ed. Joseph H. Silverman (Mexico, 1959), pp. 170–201. In a section of his introduction to the novel entitled "*El escándalo* ¿roman à clef?" Baquero Goyanes summarized most of the above points, but without adding anything really new (I, xcvii–cvi).

9. *El escándalo*, ed. M. Baquero Goyanes, II, 99–100.

10. Francisco de Paula Canalejas, "*El escándalo*, novela por Pedro A. de Alarcón," *Revista Europea*, V (July-Oct. 1875), 132–37. Canalejas's review was to have had a sequel, but if it was ever written, it was apparently never published.

11. Manuel Revilla, "Crítica literaria. *El escándalo*, por don Pedro Antonio de Alarcón," *La Ilustración Española y Americana*, XIX:2 (1875), 22–23.

12. "Bocetos literarios. D. Pedro Antonio de Alarcón," *Revista Contemporánea*, XI (1877), 17, reprinted in Revilla, *Obras* (Madrid, 1883), p. 97.

13. Leopoldo Alas, *"Doña Perfecta. Novela del Sr. Pérez Galdós,"* *El Solfeo*, no. 361, Oct. 3, 1876, reprinted in Alas, *Preludios de "Clarín,"* pp. 86–87.

14. Leopoldo Alas, *"Gloria,"* *Revista Europea*, IX (Jan.-June 1877), 209, reprinted in *Solos de Clarín*, 4th ed. (Madrid, 1891), pp. 365–66. Clarín said much the same thing in a second review of *Gloria, El Solfeo*, no. 491, Feb. 21, 1877, reprinted in *Preludios de "Clarín,"* pp. 109–11.

15. "Los novelistas españoles. Don Pedro Antonio de Alarcón," *Revista Europea*, XI (1878), 465–69, reprinted in Palacio Valdés, *Los novelistas españoles* (Madrid, 1878), pp. 49–61, and in *Semblanzas literarias* (Madrid, 1908), pp. 141–51.

16. *Apuntes y retratos literarios*, pp. 196–204.

17. P. Francisco Blanco García, *La literatura española en el siglo XIX* (Madrid, 1891), II, 458–62.

18. "Pedro Antonio de Alarcón. Juicio crítico de sus obras," *La Novela Corta*, V, no. 246 (1920).

19. César Barja, *Libros y autores modernos. Siglos XVIII y XIX* (New York, 1924), p. 434.

20. In Montesinos, *Ensayos y estudios de literatura española*, pp. 170–201.

Chapter Ten

1. *Pedro Antonio de Alarcón*, p. 180.

2. An interesting sidelight is that Robert Graves omitted this sentence in his translation of the novel. It was apparently too much for him. (*The Infant with the Globe*, trans. Robert Graves [New York, 1959], p. 5.)

3. *La Epoca*, Jan. 26, 1880.

4. Revilla's review, *"El Niño de la Bola,"* which is dated Feb. 10, 1880, was collected in *Críticas*, 1st series (Burgos, 1884), pp. 21–35.

5. Leopoldo Alas, *Solos de Clarín*, pp. 224–40.

6. Antonio de Valbuena, "Examen de libros: El Niño de la Bola, por Pedro de Alarcón," *La Ciencia Cristiana*, XIII (1880), 551–59.

7. T., *"El Niño de la Bola*, por D. Pedro A. de Alarcón," *Revista Contemporánea*, XXV (Jan.-Feb. 1880), 345–48.

8. Lais, *"El Niño de la Bola* o sea Perico Alarcón," *El Escándalo*, I, no. 2 (Jan. 31, 1880).

9. *Retratos y apuntes literarios*, pp. 204–12.

10. *Obras completas*, II, 1364.

11. Albert Bensoussan, *"El Niño de la Bola* d'Alarcón sur les planches," *Les Langues Néo-Latines*, no. 4 (Dec. 1965–Jan. 1966), 29–34. Miguel Eduardo Pardo, "Originalidad y plagio," *El Cojo Ilustrado*, VIII (1899),

97–99. Juan Valera, "Pleito literario. *El Niño de la Bola* y *Curro Vargas*," *La Ilustración Española y Americana*, LXVI:2 (1898), 364–65, reprinted in *Obras completas*, II, 983–86.

Chapter Eleven

1. Richard W. Winslow, in "The Distinction of Structure in Alarcón's *El sombrero de tres picos* and *El Capitán Veneno*," *Hispania*, XLVI (1963), 715–21, after summarizing the opinions of various critics, comes to the conclusion that *El Capitán Veneno* is truly a novel, while *El sombrero de tres picos* can more properly be considered a short story.
2. *La Iberia*, Nov. 22, 1881.

Chapter Twelve

1. *La Pródiga*, ed. A. Navarro González (Madrid, 1975), p. 51.
2. Mariano Baquero Goyanes, "*Adolphe* y *La Pródiga*," *Insula*, no. 88 (April 1953), 1, 4, 8, reprinted in *Prosistas españoles contemporáneos* (Madrid, 1956), pp. 19–31.
3. Luis Alfonso, "Estudios literarios. *La Pródiga*, novela de don Pedro Antonio de Alarcón," *Revista Hispano-Americana*, II (June 16, 1882), 600–12.
4. Servando Ruiz Gómez, "*La Pródiga* por don Pedro A. de Alarcón," *Revista de España*, LXXXVI (May-June 1882), 289–313.
5. Leopoldo Alas, "*La Pródiga*, novela de Alarcón," *La Diana*, Oct. 3, 1882, reprinted in Clarín, *Obra olvidada*, ed. Antonio Ramos-Gascón (Madrid, 1973), pp. 44–46.

Selected Bibliography

PRIMARY SOURCES

1. First Editions of Alarcón's Works, in Chronological Order

El clavo (causa célebre). Granada: M. de Benavides, 1854.

El final de Norma. 2 vols. Madrid: Fortanet, 1855.

El hijo pródigo, drama en tres actos y en verso. Madrid: José Rodríguez, 1857.

Cuentos, artículos y novelas. 3 series. Madrid: El Atalaya, 1859.

Diario de un testigo de la Guerra de Africa. Madrid: Gaspar y Roig, 1859.

De Madrid a Nápoles, pasando por París, Ginebra, etc. Madrid: Gaspar y Roig, 1861.

Novelas. Madrid: Durán, 1866.

El suspiro del moro. Canto épico. Granada: D. F. Ventura y Sabatel, 1867.

Poesías cerias y humorísticas. Madrid: Estrada, 1870.

Cosas que fueron. Colección de artículos de literatura, costumbres, crítica y viajes. Madrid: Correspondencia de España, 1871.

La Alpujarra. Sesenta leguas a caballo, precedidas de seis en diligencia. Madrid: Miguel Guijarro, 1874.

El sombrero de tres picos. Historia verdadera de un sucedido que anda en romances escrita ahora tal y como pasó. Madrid: Medina y Navarro, [1874].

El escándalo. Madrid: Medina y Navarro, 1875.

Amores y amoríos. Historietas en prosa y verso. Madrid: A. de Carlos, 1875.

Discursos leídos ante la Real Academia Española en la recepción pública del excmo. señor don Pedro Antonio de Alarcón. Madrid: V. Saiz, 1877 ("La moral en el arte").

El Niño de la Bola. Madrid: V. Saiz, 1880.

El Capitán Veneno. Madrid, 1881.

La Pródiga. Madrid: A. Pérez Dubrull, 1882.

Viajes por España. Madrid: A. Pérez Dubrull, 1883.

Juicios literarios y artísticos, Madrid: A. Pérez Dubrull, 1883.

Historia de mis libros, included in *El Capitán Veneno.* 4th ed., Madrid, 1885.

Ultimos escritos. Madrid, 1891.

2. Collections of Alarcón's Works

Definitive edition of the works prepared by the author and printed in the "Colección de Escritores Castellanos" in nineteen volumes without numeration between 1881 and 1892:

Novelas cortas I. Cuentos amatorios, 1881.
Novelas cortas II. Historietas nacionales, 1881.
Novelas cortas III. Narraciones inverosímiles, 1882.
Cosas que fueron. Cuadros de costumbres, 2nd ed., 1882.
La Alpujarra, 2nd ed., 1882.
El sombrero de tres picos, 7th ed., 1882.
La Pródiga, 1882.
El final de Norma, 5th ed., 1883.
El escándalo, 8th ed., 1883.
Viajes por España, 1883.
Juicios literarios y artísticos, 1883.
El Niño de la Bola, 3rd ed., 1884.
Poesías serias y humorísticas, 3rd ed., 1885 (includes *El hijo pródigo*).
El Capitán Veneno, 4th ed., 1885 (includes *Historia de mis libros*).
De Madrid a Nápoles, 3rd ed., 2 vols., 1885.
Ultimos escritos, 1891.
Diario de un testigo de la Guerra de Africa, 3rd ed., 2 vols., 1892.
Novelas completas. Ed. Joaquín Gil. Buenos Aires: Joaquín Gil, 1942. Contains the six novels and Catalina's biography.
Obras completas. Madrid: Fax, 1943, 1954, 1968. Contains all the material in the "Colección de Escritores Castellanos" volumes including Catalina's biography plus Martínez Kleiser's study.
Novelas completas. Madrid: Aguilar, 1974. Contains the six novels, the three volumes of short stories, *Historia de mis libros*, the academy discourse, and a prologue by Jorge Campos analyzing Alarcón's intellectual orientation.
Dos ángeles caídos y otros escritos olvidados. Ed. Agustín Aguilar y Tejera. Madrid: Imprenta Latina, 1924. Contains the previously uncollected material originally published in *El Eco de Occidente* in Granada in 1854.
Verdades de paño pardo y otros escritos olvidados. Ed. Agustín Aguilar y Tejera. Madrid: Cía. Ibero-Americana de Publicaciones, [1928]. Essentially the same material as in the previous item, although in a different order.

3. Special Editions of Alarcón's Works

"La Comendadora" y otros cuentos. Ed. Laura de los Ríos. Madrid: Ediciones Cátedra, 1975. The other stories are "El clavo," "El extran-

jero," "La mujer alta," and "El amigo de la muerte." Analyzes the five stories at some length.

El escándalo. Ed. Luis Izquierdo. Estella: Salvat Editorial, 1971. Analyzes the novel intelligently in the prologue.

El escándalo. Ed. Mariano Baquero Goyanes. "Clásicos Castellanos," 2 vols. Madrid: Espasa-Calpe, 1973. Lengthy introduction discussing Alarcón and his works, particularly *El escándalo.*

El sombrero de tres picos. Ed. Arcadio López-Casanova. Madrid: Ediciones Cátedra, 1974. With an introduction. Gives the variants.

El sombrero de tres picos. Ed. Vicente Gaos. "Clásicos Castellanos." Madrid: Espasa-Calpe, 1975. With an introduction. Lists the variants in the notes.

La Pródiga. Ed. A. Navarro González. Madrid: Editora Nacional, 1975. Good introduction to the novel.

4. English Translations Used in This Study.

The Infant with the Globe. Robert Graves, trans. New York: Thomas Yoseloff, 1959.

The Scandal. Philip H. Riley and Hubert James Tunney, trans. New York: Alfred A. Knopf, 1945.

The Three-Cornered Hat. Harriet de Onís, trans. Great Neck, N.Y.: Barron's Educational Series, 1958.

SECONDARY SOURCES

A selective list of studies on Alarcón. References to other works, usually of a more specialized nature, will be found in the Notes and References section.

BALSEIRO, JOSÉ A. *Novelistas españoles modernos.* New York: MacMillan, 1933, pp. 117–49. A rather disorganized discussion of the novels, emphasizing the Romantic elements.

BARJA, CÉSAR. *Libros y autores modernos. Siglos XVIII y XIX.* New York: G. E. Stechert, 1924, pp. 427–35. Brief, negative evaluation of Alarcón, especially of the ideological novels.

CATALINA, MARIANO. "Biografía de D. Pedro Antonio de Alarcon," in Alarcón, *Obras completas,* 3rd ed. Madrid: Fax, 1968, pp. 1899–1913. This biographical sketch was first published in 1881 as a preface to the first volume *(Cuentos amatorios)* in the "Biblioteca de Autores Castellanos" series of the *Obras completas.* Later (in 1905) Catalina continued his study on up to Alarcón's death. Since Catalina and Alarcón were close friends, this has been considered the official biography. It contains much information about Alarcón's life, but it is short on interpretation.

DE CHASCA, EDMUND. "La forma cómica en *El sombrero de tres picos*." *Hispania*, XXXVI (1953), 283–88. Useful article.

GAOS, VICENTE. "Técnica y estilo en *El sombrero de tres picos*," in *Temas y problemas de la literatura española*. Madrid: Guadarrama, 1959, pp. 179–201, reprinted in *Claves de literatura española*. Madrid: Guadarrama, 1971, I, 383–405. An intelligent analysis of the novel.

HAFTER, MONROE. "Alarcón in *El escándalo*." *Modern Language Notes*, LXXXIII (1968), 212–25. Analyzes the autobiographical elements in *El escándalo*.

HESPELT, E. H. "Alarcón as Editor of *El Látigo*." *Hispania*, XIX (1936), 319–36. Interesting article on Alarcón's relations with the paper with many quotations.

MARTÍNEZ KLEISER, LUIS. *Don Pedro Antonio de Alarcón. Un viaje por el interior de su alma y a lo largo de su vida*. Madrid: Victoriano Suárez, 1943. Reprinted as an introduction to Alarcón, *Obras completas* (Fax), pp. v–xxxii. Brief, uncritically laudatory biography. Martínez Kleiser had access to the Alarcón family archives, and he quotes material which was not previously available.

MONTESINOS, JOSÉ F. *Pedro Antonio de Alarcón*. Zaragoza: Librería General, 1955. Montesinos concentrates on Alarcón's short fiction, studying in detail the variants between the various editions. An unenthusiastic assessment of Alarcón.

————. *Pedro Antonio de Alarcón*. Madrid: Castalia, 1977. A revised and much amplified version of the previous item, which came out after this book had gone to press. Montesinos includes the article on *El escándalo* listed below and has added, among other things, chapters on *El Niño de la Bola* and *La Pródiga* plus a detailed variant study of *El final de Norma*.

————. "Sobre *El escándalo* de Alarcón," in *Ensayos y estudios de literatura española*. Ed. Joseph H. Silverman. Mexico: Andrea, 1959, pp. 170–201.

OCANO, ARMANDO. *Alarcón*. Madrid: E.P.E.S.A., 1970. The best biographical study of Alarcón.

PARDO BAZÁN, EMILIA. "Pedro Antonio de Alarcón. Necrología." *Nuevo Teatro Crítico*, I (Sept. 1891), 22–80; (Oct. 1891), 20–67; (Nov. 1891), 26–67; II (Jan. 1892), 20–54. All but the last article, "Los viajes, los artículos de costumbres, la crítica, las poesías, el drama," were reprinted in *Retratos y apuntes literarios*. Madrid: Administración, n.d., pp. 117–216. Pardo Bazán was the first to study Alarcón entire literary production in some depth. In general, sympathetic analysis.

PARDO CANALIS, ENRIQUE. *Pedro Antonio de Alarcón*. Madrid: Compañía Bibliográfica Española, 1965. In addition to a brief anthology of selections by Alarcón, it includes a useful biographical schema, a bibliography of works by and about Alarcón, and a selection of critical opinions about him.

PÉREZ GUTIÉRREZ, FRANCISCO. *El problema religioso en la generación de 1868.* Madrid: Taurus, 1975, pp. 97–129. Discusses the role played by religion in Alarcón's works, especially *El escándalo.*

REVILLA, MANUEL DE LA. "D. Pedro Antonio de Alarcón," in *Obras.* Madrid: Víctor Saiz, 1883, pp. 91–100. Discussion of Alarcón's works up through *El escándalo.*

————. *Críticas.* 1st series. Burgos: Arnaiz, 1884. Articles on *La Alpujarra, El escándalo, El Niño de la Bola,* and Alarcón's academy discourse are collected here.

RODRÍGUEZ DE LA PEÑA, H. (Julio Romano). *Pedro Antonio de Alarcón, el novelista romántico.* Madrid: Espasa-Calpe. 1933. Floridly laudatory biography.

SIMÓN DÍAZ, JOSÉ. "Bibliografía complementaria sobre autores del siglo XIX." *Revista de Literatura,* XXXI (1967), 181–95. Gives bibliographic data about where many of Alarcón's works were first published.

SORIA ORTEGA, A. "Ensayo sobre Pedro Antonio de Alarcón y su estilo." *Boletín de la Real Academia Española,* XXXI (1951), 45–92, 461–500; XXXII (1952), 119–45. Not very illuminating análysis of various works, especially *El Niño de la Bola, La Alpujarra,* and "El carbonero alcalde."

Index

(Alarcón's works are listed under his name)